HOW TO SURVIVE YOUR BOYFRIEND'S DIVORCE

HOW TO SURVIVE YOUR BOYFRIEND'S DIVORCE

*Loving Your Separated Man
Without Losing Your Mind*

ROBYN TODD AND LESLEY DORMEN

M. Evans and Company, Inc.
New York

M. Evans and Company, Inc.
216 East 49th Street
New York, New York 10017

Library of Congress Cataloging-in-Publication Data

Todd, Robyn.
    How to survive your boyfriend's divorce : loving your separated
man without losing your mind / by Robyn Todd and Lesley Dormen.
        p.   cm.
    ISBN 0-87131-922-5
    1. Divorced men—United States—Psychology.   2. Single
women—United States—Psychology.   3. Man-woman relationships—United States.   I. Dormen, Lesley.   II. Title.
HQ834.T63   1999
306.7—dc21   99-14056

Book design and typesetting by Rik Lain Schell

Printed in the United States of America

CONTENTS

ACKNOWLEDGMENTS

FIRST, OUR GRATITUDE AND thanks to the women and men who shared their personal stories, hard-won insights, and experiences with us.

We are indebted to Dr. Leslie A. Pam, Dr. Judith Sills, Dr. Jayne Migdal, Dr. Sheenah Hankin, and Dr. Jane Greer. Their thinking was crucial to our understanding of the hearts and minds of divorcing men and the women who love them. We extend that appreciation to Eleanor Alter and Raoul Felder, who shared their impressive legal experience with us.

For their ongoing support and advice, we thank Herbert Frumkes, Patti Frumkes, Mel Frumkes, Lewis Burke Frumkes, Howard Teich, Will Nix, David Levin, Ellen Lavinthal, Kathleen Freston, Jeanette Mistretta, Richard Valvo, Lee Fryd, Gregg Goldstein, William Fitzgerald, David Steinberg, Cynthia Parsons, Julia Cameron, Michele Golden, Art Harris, and Marcy Posner.

Deepest gratitude to George de Kay and his staff at M. Evans and to our agent Susan Schulman for championing this project.

Finally, a special thank-you to Ruta Fox for her early contribution to this material.

ABOUT LESLIE A. PAM, PH.D.

Leslie A. Pam, Ph.D., is a California marriage and family therapist in private practice; a former radio talk show host ("Sex and Relationships," 1994–1996, KMPC); a lecturer and seminar leader; President of the California Association of Marriage and Family Therapists, Los Angeles, 1985–1986; and the founder of Conflict Resolution Unlimited, mediating the gamut of marital, business, and other relationship disputes and negotiations. A member of the American Association of Marriage and Family Therapists, Dr. Pam has been extensively interviewed in print, radio, and television on a variety of relationship subjects. Dr. Pam is married to Marriage and Family Therapist Ann Christie, M.A., who works with him in their Los Angeles practice.

PREFACE

Several years ago, I fell in love with a man who was separated and in the process of getting a divorce. I thought, "No problem," love will conquer all. Well, it didn't. This book is the result of that roller-coaster ride. It's the road map I needed then, the guidance that might have saved my relationship, the advice that most certainly would have preserved my sanity.

In the dating world, I always considered myself pretty savvy. I never had a problem handling situations with men, and I had no reason to think this new relationship would be any different. So when friends warned me this was a whole new world and implored me to run for cover, I figured they just didn't understand my situation. It was unique, and I was special. I was convinced I could handle whatever lay ahead. But dating a man who is separated and going through a divorce turned out to be unlike any situation I had known.

Where do you go for help? My married and single girlfriends couldn't relate. I'd flipped through Oprah, Sally, and *The View* without seeing even a glimpse of my dilemma. I wanted to know how to handle myself, whether my situation was unusual, and how other women handled these same problems. I'd already stepped on a few land mines; I was frantic to avoid others that surely lay ahead. So I hauled myself to the self-help and psychology sections of every bookstore in town. I learned that men are from Mars, how to deal with stepchildren, the stages of grieving for a dead spouse. I learned how to save a marriage, how to avenge a philandering husband, how long to spend on the telephone with a new boyfriend. But I found not one sentence about how to go the distance with a not-yet-divorced man.

Eventually, I turned to a therapist. By then my once-promising relationship had crashed and burned—along with my self-esteem. I needed help putting myself back together again. Do you know how, once you've survived a romantic "war zone," you start hearing other survivors' stories? Well, I began to hear them—in great numbers. Every story was a variation of my own and involved the ex, the kids, the lawyers, the blame, the manipulations. None of those women had had a clue what to expect, either.

Now that I do, I feel compelled to share the lessons I learned with other women. If I can educate you, forewarn you, even make you laugh a little, maybe I can help you avoid some of the potholes on this particular road. While I was going through my boyfriend's divorce, I'd have given anything to read this book.

So to all you women going through your own boyfriend's divorce, the book I wanted to read is now yours.

—Robyn Todd

CHAPTER ONE

The (Almost) Perfect Man

ALL YOUR DATING LIFE, you've probably played by the rules. Like most single women, you've loved and lost, been wounded and healed, and gotten up the next morning to do it all over again. You've lived through the usual cycles of infatuation and romance, disillusionment and disappointment, the various varieties of "wrong" men, the almost-but-not-quite relationships, and the sexual and emotional droughts. You've listened politely to love advice offered by your best girlfriends, your mother, the occasional psychic, and the nice stranger at the next manicure table. For the most part, you've followed your own instincts, and they've probably served you well. You've managed to stay just this side of serious love trouble and now—armed with strength, hope, and a good haircut—you're ready to get lucky.

You never believed you wouldn't find the "right" man, not deep down. After all, men are always moving in and out of relationships, just like women. People break up. It's a sad fact that 50 percent of marriages end in divorce, but it's a not-so-sad reality that all those ex-husbands are recycling themselves at any given point in time. However, you're a person who sees the glass as half-full. You've always trusted that there was a man out there as ready for happiness as you were.

Then, miraculously, it happened. Your spunk and your staying power paid off. You met the most wonderful man! And even as your heart dared to soar, you did everything right—just the way you would with any new man. You looked both ways before flirting in his direction. You checked his ring finger. After all, you're no fool for love; you'd sooner eat beef in Britain than fall in love with a married man. You found out he's *not* married. Not really. Actually, he's In the Process of Getting a Divorce. And therein lies the problem.

Maybe it began something like this:

"It was a fix-up, but as soon as I opened the door and saw Willy's kind of shy smile and the humor in his eyes, something in me just relaxed and expanded," says thirty-four-year-old Lucy. "My friend had told me Willy and his wife had split up, that he was a wonderful guy, though not a hunk. That was fine with me. I hadn't been involved with anyone for over a year, and just meeting a nice guy sounded exactly right. We had dinner, then just walked and walked, talking and laughing, stopping somewhere for coffee. Suddenly it was three in the morning. We couldn't believe it. I couldn't stop smiling to myself. Not only did I think he was cute, he *was* wonderful—smart and sweet, and as taken with me as I was with him. Right before we said goodnight—he'd already invited me to take a drive in the country the next weekend—he confessed that this evening was particularly celebratory for him because he had filed his divorce papers that week. He looked so proud of himself. I was a little taken aback. I mean, I thought he was *already* divorced.

And then maybe you told yourself something like this:

"It seemed like a technicality. I mean, they *were* separated, had been for many months. Anyway, I'd just *met* the guy. I wasn't marrying him. And there was no question: this was a man ready for a new life. All the vibes said, 'available.' I went to sleep thinking about what to wear to the country the next weekend."

Or maybe it went something like this:

"Tim had been separated for a couple of years when we met," says thirty-year-old Kathy. I had just broken up with a longterm boyfriend. Tim was so different, so much more of a grown-up than my ex. He was close to my age, but he'd been married, he was a dad. I loved that about him. He was a serious person with responsibilities. My ex was still a baby, couldn't handle commitment, and that had been a big issue between us. Tim was completely upfront with me—he told me there were a few problems with his divorce. His wife didn't want to give up the kids, and there was a stipulation that he couldn't move out of state. But that was okay. I wasn't going anywhere. And Tim was becoming quite successful in his work—I think leaving the marriage freed up a lot of energy in that area—so he wasn't looking to uproot himself. He was just concerned that she'd want more money."

And so maybe you thought something like this:

"Obviously there were a few mild little unpleasantries. But the main thing was, they'd been separated for quite a while now. Tim was available, no question. And he insisted the worst was behind him. I figured, my timing is good. There's light at the end of the tunnel, he's at the end of the process. All that's left really is the legal stuff. The actual divorce should take very little time. I couldn't wait to meet his kids."

Or maybe you told yourself, "Love will prepare me for whatever is to come":

"Lee was battle-scarred, just emerging from a horrific sixteen-year marriage," says Rebecca, an artist in her early thirties. "He was kind of standing there, disoriented and blinking in the sun." Mutual friends had introduced her to the forty-year-old entertainment executive. "He'd just filed for separation. You've never seen a more miserable man. I knew he had some recovering to do. But you know what? Even at his most miserable Lee was the most exciting, most alive and stimulating man I'd ever been with." He fell hard for Rebecca, too. "He kept telling me I was beyond his wildest dreams, that I was his reward for finally walking out of that darkness. When I was with him I felt like my very finest, my very best self. I could see him starting to come back to life again. We found each other. It was that simple."

It's not as if you didn't see a few problems ahead:

Marie, a twenty-eight-year-old assistant to a movie star, met Carl, a real estate mogul, at a wedding. "Ours was a long-distance relationship—I lived in Los Angeles, he lived in Chicago—so that presented difficulties," says Marie. "But within a month, we knew we had something special. Carl had only been married for five years, and he was in the midst of the divorce process. I figured, a year at the most. Then, after he'd settled everything in as favorable a way as possible, we'd get on with our lives. I worried most about the geographical obstacle, but I tried to see the up side. Time would go by that much faster."

No matter what the situation, you always kept your inner dialogue cheerful and optimistic. You told yourself:

- A good man is hard to find.

- We have this amazing connection—that's rare in this world.

- This is a man who *wants* to be married. He just married the wrong woman.

- He's physically out of the house, so my timing is actually good.

- The divorce will force us to go slow, and slow is always better.

- Love is always about taking a risk.

So it's kind of a bummer when your best friend and your mother look like that painting "The Scream" and tell you:

● Run as fast as you can in the opposite direction.

● Tell him to throw your number in the garbage and call you in two years.

WHY THE PEOPLE WHO LOVE YOU SAY, "GET OUT NOW!"

Because that's their job—to protect you from love's worst-possible scenarios. Falling in love with a separated, not-quite-divorced man is one of love's worst-possible scenarios.

Why?

"Each divorce is the death of a small civilization," says novelist Pat Conroy. Read that sentence again. Sure, half of all marriages fail. But a civilization—even a small one—is something else entirely. A civilization isn't created by a piece of paper and a handful of rice. A marriage may end, but a civilization has rituals and cultures, monuments and history, habits and memories. When it dies, it leaves its inhabitants stunned, bewildered, and angry.

Need another metaphor? "Divorce is like a huge boulder crashing into a small pond," says Dr. Judith Sills, a Philadelphia clinical psychologist. "It creates a wave. That wave takes a lot of people down with it."

If you've been married yourself, you already know what happens when a civilization dies, when that tsunami of grief and anger crashes upon your personal shore. Or maybe you forgot. The point is, you're lovely and frisky and full of hope right now. "Not me," you tell the naysayers. "I can handle it."

WHAT THIS BOOK WILL TELL YOU

This book isn't your girlfriend or your mother. This book accepts the following reality: real women *do* fall·in love with men who haven't completely extricated themselves from their former lives. Some of those women manage to love those men, and to be loved by them, without being psychically flattened or sacrificing their precious emotional sanity in the process. Some of those women go on to marry those men. Like you, this book sees the glass as half-full. It says it is possible to love the man who is leaving a marriage without nuking your self-esteem in the process. Other women have done it. You can do it, too.

But first you must ask yourself three crucial questions:

Am I the Kind of Woman Who Is Willing to Take This Risk?

Don't kid yourself. That's exactly what you're about to do: take a risk. A not-quite-divorced man is high-risk love. No, not quite as high-risk as an affair with a married man. But way, *way* up there. Yes, taking a risk means putting yourself in the path of happy opportunity. And taking a risk also means increasing the possibility of pain. After all, that's the definition of risk.

So are you the kind of woman who is willing to take this risk?

Well, have you ever been in a relationship like this before? If so, did you spend six months weeping, a year or so in therapy, or did you deplete your bank account or derail your career in the process? You might want to ask yourself if you're prepared to revisit that particular experience.

But remember, you may lie to yourself. It's human nature. It's tough to be objective, and few of us can do it. Our wish to move forward is just too powerful.

Is He the Kind of Man Worth Taking a Risk Over?

If dating a single man is Dating 101, dating a separated man is dating on a graduate level—like, doctorate. Most of us never get past Dating 101, even though we should. More often than not, we evaluate a guy by how nicely he treats the waiter, by what our nervous system says when he nuzzles our ear, by whether we're absolutely positive we knew him in another life. This is not that. Graduate dating is not about asking yourself, "How does he make me feel?" It's about asking, "Who has he been in this world? What have his relationships been like? What is there about this man that suggests to me that I *should* take such a big risk? What is it about him that gives me confidence? What is it about him that could reduce—or, alternately—increase the risk?" Here are some guidelines that Dr. Sills and others point to:

- If he has been married a long time, if he left his wife a couple times before but never totally completed the process, if he's had a series of affairs, or if he's clearly had commitment issues all along, he's more of a risk than a man whose wife wants to leave or who has been forced to complete some of that separation process before he met you.

- Did he move out last week, or are the papers already filed? Have significant family members and friends been informed? Again, it's a question of greater and lesser risk. Not that one answer suggests an absolute "Go for it," and another indicates a certain recipe for disaster. More to the point, it's about being clear-eyed about what you're taking on, about listening to your head as well as your heart, and about being as brutally honest as possible with yourself about the risk you're preparing to take.

Of course, there's another problem here. Men in this situation routinely lie. He'll lie to himself, and he'll lie to you. He'll say, "I'm a heartbeat away from a divorce" when the fact is he just walked out and hasn't worked up the nerve to file because he knows that once he does his wife's wrath will fall on his head. Lucy, whose blind date with Willy led to a wonderful weekend in the country followed by three years of anguish, knows this one well. "He said they'd been separated for five months when in fact she'd been in a psychiatric hospital for that long, ever since he left, and he was still telling her he was reconsidering things," says Lucy. "The part I didn't get for another year was that he drove her there."

Sometimes a man asks his lawyer to help him lie to his girlfriend, says prominent divorce lawyer Raoul Felder. "He'll insist to his girlfriend that his wife is stalling him, but it's in his interest to stretch out the divorce so that he doesn't have to pay a large sum of money until the end of the case. Most lawyers won't lie. But given how overloaded the court system is, it's not hard to jerk a case around for a couple of years if that's what you want to do."

Chances are good that your separated sweetie isn't in much of a hurry. Once a man is separated, he tends to stall out. He's comfortable there. He doesn't want to stir the hornet's nest.

That said, it's up to you to ask questions, ask follow-up questions, ask follow-ups to the follow-ups, and listen between the lines. As of this writing, there are no polygraphs distributed with restaurant menus. There is no sodium pentothal available behind the counter with the condoms. It's up to you to open your mouth and ask the questions that you will then, along with a big grain of salt, file away for further consideration. Yes, you will glean information about his favorite movies and his childhood and whether the idea of bicycling through Tuscany appeals to him or if he prefers hanging out on the beach. But you will also need to ask:

● Who initiated the separation?

● Was there infidelity? Whose?

● What does he think went wrong with the marriage?

● What reasons does he think his wife would give for what went wrong?

● Does he hope for a reconciliation? Does she?

● Has he hired a lawyer, filed papers, or told the kids?

● Does he envision a custody fight or a battle over the settlement? Does she?

So go ahead, evaluate his decorating aesthetic, his attitude toward his mother, and his sense of humor, but circle hawklike right back to his marriage and his wife and the state of his divorce. And don't forget that grain of salt, the kosher kind.

No one says, "I'm dating a man who's getting divorced from a decent woman who was a great mom, and it's not clear what the reasons are but he just seems to want a fresh start." That view of divorce is intolerable to a woman. Therefore, every separated man was married to a witch who tortured him, stole his money, lived off him in a vile and immoral way while he single-handedly raised the children, and with whom he suffered and struggled due to his essential integrity and moral goodness.

So what he'll tell you will probably sound something like this:

● They haven't had sex in five years. (Explanation for the three-year-old she's suing him for custody of: "Pity sex.")

● He married her because his parents/society/her parents forced him.

- She's terminally ill.

- She's clinically depressed and mentally unbalanced.

- She's recovering from being terminally ill or clinically depressed or mentally unbalanced.

- She abuses him/the children/the help/the pets.

- He'd be divorced by now but he's been waiting for the kids to finish school/start school/move out of the house/or for his mother to die.

- She's an alcoholic/drug addict/lesbian—or all of these things.

- She's cold, fat, critical, boring, controlling, suicidal—or all of these things.

- He didn't want to fork over his entire net worth in a settlement.

You may end up picturing his wife/ex-wife as a combination of:

- Camilla Parker Bowles

- Joan Collins

- A prison matron in a 1940s film noir

And how she pictures you, even if she doesn't know you exist, or even if you don't exist is:

- Glenn Close, in *Fatal Attraction*

So is he worth the risk, even with the knowledge that the man who sits before you is an optical illusion? Because weirdly enough, as he pours you another glass of wine, laughs at your jokes, stares thoughtfully into your eyes as you ask your frank questions and consider his seemingly genuine and straightforward answers, you do not see a frightened, lying, desperate, guilty, hanging-on-by-his-fingernails almost-survivor of a cataclysmic devastation. You do not see a man who has recently had a near-death experience and is reliving it even now as he seems to be discussing his passion for golf. Instead you see an open-hearted, emotionally vulnerable, sexually starved, adoring husband-without-a-mate. Compared to all those commitment-shy, never-married guys you've loved, the ones who start hyperventilating when you casually mention plans for the weekend, this man seems heavensent. He's *been* married (and, by the way, still is). He has fathered children, changed diapers, played catch. He's a family man. Not *your* family man, of course, but it's just a matter of time and a few legal details. You see the divorce as a thing of the past, a *fait accompli*. You see him as free and emotionally available.

And your heart goes out to him.

Reel it right back in.

How Can I Minimize the Risk?

If you were planning to climb Mt. Everest, what would you do? You'd assess whether you were capable of the challenge, invest in all the best safety equipment, hire a guide, and make sure you were in the best physical shape of your life. If you were thinking of investing in a high-risk stock, you'd objectively evaluate the odds and weigh the potential gains with your ability to absorb the potential loss. In other words, you'd do everything you could to familiarize yourself with the risk and then take whatever precautions possible to minimize it.

There are climbers who take all the precautions and never make it to the summit—some lose their lives trying. There are high-risk investors who make millions and many more who become paupers. Whenever you take a big risk, the chances of failure are great; you can't guarantee success.

But you *can* minimize the risk. This book will tell you how. It will be your guide, your ally, your blueprint, your reality check. Sometimes strict, sometimes forgiving, but always on your side, this book will help you read between the lines of your boyfriend's behavior and your own. It will tell you how to present yourself and how to preserve yourself. It will always keep *your* best interests in mind. There will be times when you can't do that, when you won't want to do that. This book will arm you with the information that can help keep you honest with yourself.

What Else You'll Need

A solid good friend to confide in and turn to for support. A video store to help with the self-pity and the downtime. A gym to help you deal with the anger.

And This. . .

The knowledge that, starting now and at any given time during the days and weeks to come, you will *always* have three options:

- You can bail out of the relationship.

- You can put the relationship on hold.

- You can continue with the relationship.

CHAPTER TWO

At Long Last Love (and Its Evil Twin)

I N THE MOVIES YOU always know exactly when new lovers bond blissfully into a couple-in-love. That's when you get the lovers' montage, that syrupy visual sequence where you see them laughing in the sun, nuzzling in the rain, offering each other licks of their ice cream cones, riding a Ferris wheel, gazing dreamily into each others' eyes over candlelight. Sure, your average real-life couple looks and feels as blissed out as that idyllic movie couple—if you edit out a few details.

Like the moment one or both begins to panic because they don't know where all this feeling will lead or if they want it to lead anywhere.

Like the time they make love and afterwards she says, "You seem distant, what are you thinking?" and he says "Nothing."

Like each of their romantic resumes and idiosyncratic fears—his inability to have ever made a serious commitment to a woman so far in his life or her reluctance to trust a man because her last boyfriend cheated on her.

Like the obstacles and complications that two ordinary people bring to a relationship even when they are both totally free and available—they live in different states, or they each have kids from previous marriages. Like the accommodations all perfectly ordinary couples struggle to make to each other. Can she really live with his neurotic obsession with sports? Will her insistence on taking cabs everywhere lead to his financial ruin?

In other words, if you edit out the flip side of love, even a *normal* relationship has a dark side, an anti-relationship, an evil twin lurking in the shadows, waiting to leap out when you least expect it, ready to spoil the happy lovers' montage.

RECOGNIZING THE EVIL TWIN

When you fall in love with a separated man, the evil twin is *really* evil. Not only are you likely to be ambushed by the usual love devils, you also get a cast of troublemakers utterly unique to your situation. These devils trip you up because they're invisible. They blindside you because you've never encountered them before and aren't looking for them. They jump out and say "Gotcha!" just when you think you're the happiest, luckiest, most serene gal you've ever been.

See if you can spot the devils in the following conversation.

"I feel blessed," Rebecca tells her best friend Alison over lunch. Her face glows as she leans conspiratorially across the table. "I'm in love, Al, really in love. Lee is the most considerate, most conscientious, most attentive man I've ever been involved with. He wants to be with me all the time. He met me at a shoe sale yesterday in Bloomingdale's."

"Uh-huh," says Alison, one eyebrow raised in the skeptical position it has assumed ever since Rebecca began offering these carbonated accounts of rapturous sex and soulful connection three weeks ago.

"Really, Al, you'll love him. He's smart, funny, sexy, sweet. . ."

"Married."

"Oh, come on, he's filed for divorce. He'd be divorced already if that harridan weren't torturing him over the settlement. He's way too generous, and she just loves to punish him. But don't get me started on *her*. Did I tell you he invited me skiing in February? This weekend we're looking at apartments. He wants his new place to be something I love."

"I thought you were going on one of those Earthwatch trips in February."

"Well, I can do that any time," says Rebecca. Just then the cell phone in her purse begins to chirp. Digging for it, Rebecca offers her friend a sheepish smile. "Lee gave it to me so I'd always be reachable. 'Hi, sweetie. I know, I miss you too. I'm having the grilled chicken Caesar. Did you eat yet?'"

Alison watches her friend's face wilt, droop, deflate.

"Oh, darling, that's okay. Of course we can do it another night. I love you, too." Rebecca clicks off. Sighs.

"You look like one of those time-lapse flower films in reverse," says Alison. "What's wrong?"

"We were supposed to have dinner tonight to celebrate my pro-motion, but his wife is making him come over to discuss financing the kids' orthodontia or something." Rebecca glowers. "That bitch."

"Why didn't he tell her he had plans tonight?" says Alison. "I mean, they're separated. It's not like you two are having an affair."

"Are you kidding? She doesn't know about me! Lee asked me to keep it a secret so it wouldn't totally screw up the settlement. I'm not even supposed to be telling you. Anyway, he said he'd try to come over after." Rebecca's face brightened. "Did I tell you how he loves to make me breakfast in the morning?"

THE DEVIL: IT FEELS LIKE A MARRIAGE EVEN THOUGH IT'S NOT

Rebecca has known Lee for three weeks, but she feels as if she's known him three years. Rebecca knows Lee's worries, guilts, and fears almost as well as her own. She's fully intimate with the details of his digestive system, the problems his little daughter Julia has getting to sleep at night, the secrets of his marital bed. Rebecca and Lee fell in love fast. They speak three times a day. They've slipped effortlessly into the married couple rhythm of things. Rebecca feels more than infatuated, more than in love—she feels bonded to this man. Lee doesn't just love her, he needs her. This is what she's always wanted—not to be swept off her feet, but to be swept into this daily, boring, wonderful exchange of trivia, feeling, history, laughter. She's never met a man this willing to let her so far in. Rebecca knows that she and Lee have a brilliant future ahead of them.

She couldn't be more wrong.

That's how it goes with separated men. In fact, you'd think someone would have figured out how to bottle whatever it is these guys give off in order to sell it to dateless single guys and make a zillion dollars. A separated man couples with mate-for-life intensity and speed. There are reasons for this. One is that he hasn't had even halfway decent sex since early in the first Clinton Administration, and he is so grateful for it and for you that he'd like to name a national holiday and a couple of schools after you—let alone fall in love. Another is that he knows the value of a genuine intimate connection with a woman. Maybe he has been separated long enough to have had that first liberating but ultimately disappointing flurry of dates and has come to realize that meeting a woman you can take to bed and happily spend the whole next day with is a small miracle. Here are some of the things he's telling you now:

● You're so beautiful.

● No one understands me as well as you do.

● I've never felt so comfortable with anyone.

● You are exactly my type.

- If I'd met you first, I'd have married you.

- We have all the same interests.

- I've never felt this powerful an attraction to anyone, ever.

- You are amazing.

- I'm glad you're so happy, upbeat, thin, supportive,
  fashionable, spontaneous.

- I'm glad you like sex so much.

And yes, you are all those things and more. Nonetheless, the force driving his devotion right now is his desperation to reattach. As in, he needs that attachment in order to survive. Do you for one moment think a man who wasn't desperate would go to a shoe sale in Bloomingdale's? That's your guy. As horribly insane or dull as dirt his relationship with his wife has become, marriage is a lifeline to a man. Literally. Medical and psychological studies tell us that married men are happier, healthier, jauntier, jollier. Men without wives? All around sicker, sadder, deader. While we women have been gaslit into believing that connection-for-life is in our DNA, the fact is, men are the ones who can't survive without mar-riage. Marriage is very comfortable for men, and a separated man will instinctively seek to recreate its cozy rhythms with the first woman he even remotely cares for. He will offer you intensity, intimacy, reassurance, and future talk, not to mention a pile of shirts for the laundry. And you didn't even have to ask.

And you? You like intensity. You like intimacy. Reassurance is one of your most favorite things. You are very much in favor of marriage in general. The ease with which the two of you have slipped into this warm bath of love and closeness astounds and delights you. You've dated never-married men. You are familiar with the wall those men put up, with the difficulty in getting through that wall to anywhere resembling a place you'd remotely like to be. You've analyzed that wall within an inch of its life. That wall is Siberia. This warmth is St. Bart's. What woman in her right mind would trade this warmth for that wall?

But here's a question to ask yourself: Did you ever stop to think that the wall might be appropriate?

Why This Devil Is Dangerous

If Rebecca were dating an unmarried man, she'd probably think there was something screwy about so much intensity so quickly. Instinctively she'd be pulling back, wondering why the guy was so pathetically needy. Your basic smart, garden-variety neurotic grown-up is wise enough to know that falling in love is prologue, that when the air clears after all those flashy fireworks, the actual relationship is just beginning. The wall we all put up at the start of a romance is intelligently self-protective. We know that if we give ourselves over, body and soul, we might be setting ourselves up for a fall.

We get lost in the fantasy and often get our hearts broken when we have to face the fact that this person is not a good match for us, Dr. Sheenah Hankin, a clinical psychologist, points out. Once the prologue is over, we might not even be interested enough to continue the story. That's courtship in a nutshell. We fear intimacy as passionately as we crave it. It's human nature. It's the tension in the boy-gets-girl, boy-loses-girl, boy-gets-girl-back-again roller coaster of romance. And vice versa. We love those stories because we recognize ourselves and all our contradictions in them.

When you fall in love with a separated man, something is missing. It's the fear. He doesn't seem to have any. He's one big welcoming embrace, like a sunny sky right before a hideous tornado sucks up everything in its path. Not that you actually see the color of the sky. "It was Paul's voice I was falling in love with," says thirty-nine-year-old Katie, who met forty-five-year-old Paul a year and a half after his separation, on a walking tour in the Cotswalds. "When we got home, we talked for hours every night on the phone. I'd never met a man so easily, cozily intimate. There were no walls, none. We just started talking and didn't stop. I wasn't used to that in my dating life. He'd been married for twenty years. That was the only way he knew how to talk to a woman. It was irresistible. On the other hand, his divorce was still over a year away from happening."

There's something off, though, about a divorcing man's absence of natural caution. Not only is it unnatural, it's dangerous as well. It means that the only grown-up around is you. You're the one who has to take the long view. You're the one who has to supply the caution for both of you.

Why? Because at some point his fear *will* kick in. And where will you be? Speeding downhill emotionally at breakneck speed. It's not only your heart you're protecting, it's also your potential future as a couple. At some point, he's going to look at you and panic. He's going to think, *I must be out of my mind to rush into a serious relationship right on the heels of my divorce.* When whatever made him leave his wife or whatever made his wife leave him gets transferred to you.

It isn't easy to be cautious. It takes tremendous effort to hold on to yourself. Nonetheless, you have to be the realist, the one with open eyes. His desire to be with you and to go forward is genuine, but he doesn't have the ability to make it happen. He's smitten on one level, scared on another. He's never met anyone like you, but he's still caught up in the pain, shock, and denial of what went on in his marriage. And that's particularly true if there was a betrayal, say a number of marital therapists.

How to Protect Yourself

When Marie, the assistant to a movie star, met Carl at a wedding in Los Angeles, she was smitten by the tall, good-looking businessman. At the end of the evening, they knew they wanted to see each other again. The only problem was, Carl lived in Chicago. "We had that first promising evening, then brunch the next day, then he was gone." Marie couldn't tell which she felt more intensely—relief or disappointment. Over brunch, Carl told her he'd recently separated from his wife after five years of marriage. "I kind of closed my ears to the details from the minute I heard that. I knew he had a road to travel, plus he didn't live in my city. Mentally I crossed him off as boyfriend material." But the attraction was undeniable. Over the next month they spoke on the phone often. "He talked about his marriage, and I listened. We talked about a million other things. We laughed a lot. We got to know each other." Carl flew to Los Angeles about six weeks after they first met. "It was great to see him, but I promised myself that I wouldn't sleep with him. I knew that once we were lovers I'd expect more."

As their telephone relationship continued, Marie made it clear to Carl that she didn't want to hear the details of his divorce. "I asked the big questions: Have you filed the papers, and how long do you expect it will take. I don't want the play-by-play. I don't want to be emotionally invested in the settlement. The way I see it, we're dating. Period." They have continued to see each other intermittently. They've also become lovers. But geography is in Marie's favor. It's helping her do what you'll have to do through determination alone. "He's not around, so I can't get more enmeshed than I should," says Marie. "My life continues as always—friends, work, the occasional date. Carl is an extra, something I hope has a future, but I'm not counting on it. I can't. There's still room here for disappointment. He's not divorced."

While geography has helped Marie protect herself, there are other things you can do to keep from falling headfirst into a relationship with a separated man.

Stay skeptical. So you're not lucky enough to have a continent between you? Then you'll have to set the limits yourself. But how do you do that when your heart and your hormones are conspiring against you? Channel Jack Webb. Jack Webb was the detective on that classic TV show *Dragnet*, famous for his deadpan, "Just the facts, Ma'am" approach to crime. That's you. When the love stuff really gets going is exactly when you need to get in touch with your inner Jack Webb. When he says the divorce is a done deal, when he promises eternal devotion, when he implores you to stay the course and be a good soldier, smile Mona Lisa-like and let him know you appreciate the optimistic words. But inside, your response should be, "Yeah. Right. Whatever."

Valerie, forty, is dating Paul, a wonderful guy she met at a medical convention. Paul told her he was "as good as divorced" the first night they had dinner; he was signing the papers in "a week or so." It is now eight months later, and the divorce is ongoing. "I love this man, and we have a wonderful time together," says Valerie, "but I don't allow him to discuss anything remotely resembling our future together. I remind him, very matter-of-factly, that he's a married man. I won't take a vacation with him, I won't meet his kids, I don't tell him what I do when we're not together." Valerie projects this attitude: You can talk the talk, but if you don't walk the walk, I can't take you seriously. Valerie isn't blessed with superior genetic self-control, but she is savvy. "Sure, I'm frustrated and angry, but I don't let him see that," she says. "If I think I'm going to be tempted to have an angry conversation with him, I leave my answering machine on. If I feel myself starting to feel clingy and insecure, I call a girlfriend." Valerie hasn't given Paul an ultimatum—yet—but she has put herself on notice. "If the divorce isn't final by the one-year mark, I'm breaking it off."

Ask: *Is he out of the house?* Don't even think of becoming sexually involved with him unless he has moved out, established a separate residence, and filed divorce papers. Tell him to call you once all those steps have been taken. Otherwise you'll be tugging at him: When are you going to move out? Did you call the lawyer yet? Even if he has established a separate residence, you are not enabling the divorce. Enabling the divorce does not necessarily lead to enabling a marriage. Katya, a thirty-three-year-old math teacher, wished she had followed that advice when she fell in love with Alex, a colleague. "We were good friends, so I knew a lot about the ongoing trouble in his marriage," she says. "Our friendship became romantic after he made the decision to leave the marriage and, to be honest, it took us both by surprise." They became lovers. "I thought the decision was the big thing, then telling her. But he was still there, sleeping on the couch." Meanwhile, sexual intimacy upped the emotional stakes for Katya: "It always does, so I should have known better." Alex's wife insisted they enter therapy together. "He was convinced it would help her get through the divorce," says Katya. Instead it slowed the divorce process down to the speed of continental drift and turned Katya into a shrew. "I saw him every day, and all I could see was this enraging passivity. The relationship just self-destructed." Katya wound up taking a job at another school. Alex's divorce became final two years later, and he is now remarried.

Be empathic, not enmeshed. Distance yourself from the center of the storm of his divorce. Therapists warn that the worst scenario is that the two of you have a torrid affair, he leaves his wife, then moves in with you. You'll be there for every microsecond of his rage and guilt. You'll be going through the divorce with him, except at the end he'll be divorced. But what will you be? The transitional girlfriend, most likely. Statistics tell us that most men who have affairs before they leave their marriages don't wind up marrying their affair partner. Angela, forty-two, calls it "sick room syndrome" after having gone through such an experience. "When you're right there in the middle of it all, you become indelibly associated with the misery of it. He's at his weakest, his guiltiest, his angriest, and you've seen him that way. When he's strong again, that image of himself will still be associated with you and chances are he'll hate you for it."

Penny, thirty-five, whose romance with just-divorced attorney Frank crashed and burned after eight months, saw herself turning into Frank's wife. "All along he'd been telling me horror stories about this woman: she was insane, out-of-control, a total maniac.

By the end of those eight months, I understood exactly why. That's who I'd become. On one of our last evenings together, we went to dinner. Walking into the restaurant, Frank spotted some friends of his wife at a table. As we walked to our table, he stopped and introduced me as 'Barbara.' Barbara? When we sat down, I just lost it. He denied even doing it, started telling me I was out of control—I *was* out-of-control. We'd been living together for two months, I didn't even meet the man until he and his wife had separated, and he was automatically still treating me like a mistress. I wound up throwing a plate at him! Me. I'd never done anything like that in my life. We limped along another couple months, and then broke up. I was as crazy and demanding as his wife, he said."

You think you've seen him through the worst, nursed him through the worst, and that at the end of the illness he'll be devoted to you? Guess again. He'll want a fresh start with someone who doesn't know that he's capable of being such a pitiful wreck.

Let him handle the business of his divorce before you think of yourself as a couple. He'll need a support, one person who knows every detail, one person he calls when he gets off the phone with his ex or comes home from the lawyer's office and needs to rant. If you're that person or want to be, *you* need to have a best friend supporting you—and it can't be him. Chances are you'll hate that best friend, because she'll be doing a lot of reality testing. It's one of the reasons we pull away from friends in situations like this.

Don't pay for him. A lot of women feel sorry for their boyfriend because the divorce is draining him financially. Big mistake. Go ahead and feel sorry, but don't take care of him financially. Marianne, thirty-five, resumed a college romance with Joe when he decided to leave his five-year-old marriage. "I was doing well financially and he wasn't, so I let him move in with me temporarily until he got on his feet. I paid for everything, including making it possible for his young daughter to visit us from out-of-state where she lived with her mother." Marianne's generosity quickly turned controlling. Now that she had a financial stake in the guy

as well as an emotional stake, she couldn't stand watching him
dither around with his lawyer, with his wife, with her. "I was pissed
off all the time," she says. At Christmas, Joe's wife came to town
with their daughter, the only way she'd let him see the girl.
Marianne financed their stay at a hotel. "On Christmas Eve day he
called me from the hotel and said he'd decided to stay with them,
that divorce was too expensive."

Even if he's the one who's flush, be prepared to pay for yourself
anyway. "If he's spending a lot of money on you, there's going to
be a problem because half of that money belongs to his wife," says
matrimonial attorney Eleanor Alter. She always advises the girlfriend to go Dutch to some degree. "Don't let him buy you big
jewelry. If he's telling his wife he can't give her money for a nice
vacation this summer and she finds out he's taken his girlfriend to
Italy for two weeks, there's going to be trouble." It's a red flag, and
a judge isn't going to like it, says Alter. Especially where money is
tight. "Don't go unless you can pay your own way," she advises.
"It's all marital money until there's an agreement. That's hard in
the relationship, but it's real. Know it upfront." Are you the kind
of woman for whom Hermes and two weeks at a four-star Parisian
hotel spell true love? Then be prepared to foot the bill. Or find
yourself a single boyfriend.

Employ the Ninety-Day Rule. We'd like to pass along Dr. Hankin's
heartbreak avoidance plan—modeled after job tryouts and appli-
ance warranties—which she created for all her single clients. If
you're dating a separated man, it's got your initials all over it.

- No falling in love—that is, declaring love to the
  other, telling your friends you are in love—until
  after ninety days.

- During this three-month period, do a lot of
  research about the kind of person you are
  involved with. Find out about his past relation-

ships and any problems involved with those. If possible, meet his friends. Share all of these things about yourself.

- Make no plans together beyond the ninety days. Book no vacations or agree to go to weddings or to spend holidays beyond that period.

- Don't give up your friends or your activities. Keep your life going as usual outside the relationship.

In short, if you're restocking your lingerie drawer, refusing dates from eligible men, buying resort wear, and having more than your usual number of pedicures and bikini waxes, stop at once. If you're neglecting your career and your friends, refusing to travel solo, reading books on how to be a good stepmother, and canceling all social plans to be available to him at a moment's notice, cease and desist. That's the devil making you do it.

THE DEVIL: IT FEELS LIKE AN AFFAIR EVEN THOUGH IT'S NOT

When Lee told Rebecca that he didn't want their romance public knowledge until his divorce was settled, she understood. They had just finished making love. "You're very important to me," he told her, stroking her hair. "We have to be discreet. I don't want anything to get in the way of our future. Once my wife knows I'm seeing someone, she'll do everything she can to slow the divorce down." Before long, Rebecca's understanding was at odds with her natural inclinations. She had told her friends and family about the wonderful new man she was falling love with, and she wanted Lee to meet them. "Let's wait," he told her. Despite the warm, loving, fun times they spent together going to movies and the theater, eating in restaurants, and playing tennis, there were subtle lines being drawn. "We had to avoid certain restaurants because his wife's friends might see us," Rebecca says. "We had to avoid certain neighborhoods and tennis clubs because his daughter or one of her friends might see us." The cell phone Lee gave her quickly began to be an instrument of torture. "He had to cancel or rearrange our plans all the time because his wife or the kids needed something from him."

Jane, a thirty-four-year-old single mother, says her separated boyfriend Ted raced home to his place every night after their dates, even after being separated close to a year. "He claimed to be uncomfortable sleeping over because of my daughter, but the real reason was that he wanted to be there to take his wife's late-night calls. They were in the middle of the negotiation, and he didn't want to risk her anger by revealing his new relationship. He said it was temporary, but I felt crummy inside, like I was doing something wrong."

Your natural impulse is to normalize your relationship. Instead you feel as though you're having an affair with a married man. Well, my sweet, you are. And if you're determined to be married yourself sometime within the next two years, dump this guy and look elsewhere.

That said, it's a matter of how much secrecy you can or should tolerate before it starts eating away at your self-esteem. Secrecy can cost you your emotional well-being. Sometimes it's required, but you don't give away parts of your soul and you don't isolate yourself for love alone. That's trading way too much.

How do you know whether or not to go along with a clandestine affair? You're the only one who can make that call. Sherry, forty, was a massage therapist in the process of leaving a childless, four-year marriage when she met fifty-year-old Evan through a mutual friend. They connected immediately. Evan had only just separated from his wife of twenty-four years. He had two children, fifteen and nineteen. Soon after Sherry and Evan met, Sherry left her marriage and moved into a small apartment. Evan's lawyer told him to stay in his house for the time being, so as not to inflame his wife as their divorce conversations continued. He was not to let on that he'd met a new woman. Evan and Sherry saw each other at her apartment exclusively. This went on for six months. "I told my closest girlfriend and that was it," says Sherry. "It was tough not going out in public, but I recognized that it was necessary. Plus, I was going through my own divorce. It was a cleaner divorce than Evan's, but I was making my own adjustments." After six months of clandestine dating, Evan moved out, filed for divorce, and found a place of his own. They no longer had to be a secret. "Still, I knew in my heart that it would be a good three years before Evan was free and clear, and I was determined to wait it out," says Sherry. It was a tentative time. "Once his wife knew about us, shortly after Evan moved out, she became a lot less cooperative. The first six months were the hardest because Evan was still going through the motions of trying to save his marriage, seeing a therapist, taking his wife on vacation. It wasn't the secrecy so much as the fact that I really felt I was having an affair. Even after he left, I told myself it would probably be a three-year ordeal. I was determined to wait it out." The divorce was finalized in two and a half years. Sherry and Evan were married three years after they met.

How to Protect Yourself

Accept secrecy for a limited period of time. If he says, "my lawyer says not to make it public until the divorce goes through," this is what you say: "I need to understand that. What do you mean by secret? Do you mean not in public?" Don't give yourself away. If you're forbidden to tell anyone for a year or more, let him make it worth your while financially—you're investing your time and emotions with him, and he ought to prove he has a vested interest in you, too. If he won't do that, tell him: "I love you, I want a relationship with you, but the best way to guarantee that your money is safe is not to call me until it is."

Should you speak with his lawyer? If your relationship is serious, consider it. Many women do. "Tell him you'd like to speak to the lawyer alone, then pay for the consultation yourself," suggests attorney Raoul Felder. Many therapists agree. Tell him that you'd like to get a clear picture of the time frame from the lawyer, that you're only interested in the part that concerns you. If the two of you haven't made any commitment to each other, you probably won't go that route. Your only gauge right now is how long a divorce "usually" takes and how willing your boyfriend and his lawyer are to level with you about how long it actually is taking.

If he avoids the topic, shuts you down when you want to discuss it, or patronizes you by saying it's not a problem, beware. If he makes you a flurry of promises, then doesn't follow through because his wife or kids made some demand on him, he's far more entrenched than he realizes and it's going to be difficult. More positive signs? He sets limits around his availability and accessibility to his wife and kids, and then sticks by them. He's willing to talk openly with you and answer your questions about where the divorce process is at. He's willing to get support and guidance from a therapist if necessary.

If You Decide to Continue. . .

Remember, you're still in the honeymoon stage of your romance. You think he's wonderful, and he adores you. You haven't met the kids yet, though they sound darling. But you haven't felt the full force of his fear and his panic. His wife probably doesn't know you exist. You are barely acquainted with the glacial pace of the legal system and the lawyers who gum it up. You've made some tiny compromises, but nothing too terrible to swallow. Mostly you're accommodating and sweet. You have great sex, hang out well together, enjoy the same things. You never fight. There's enough turmoil going on in the rest of his life.

On the other hand, you're beginning to become aware that his problems seem to dominate your conversations. As in, the minute you say, "How are you?" you get an epic earful of some brand-new drama. When you have a problem or a crisis, you think twice about burdening him with it. You'd really like him to meet your friends and your family. It would be nice to be having a regular dating life.

Still, he is saying things like, "It's only a matter of time" or "I can't wait until it's over" or "We're in the home stretch now."

Be prepared to hear these homilies for another year or two.

HOW ARE YOU DOING?
An Emotional Sanity Checklist

Do three or more of the following statements describe you or your boyfriend? If so, enlist a friend or therapist to help you end the relationship or put it on hold.

○ 1. You can't concentrate at work.

○ 2. You've canceled social plans, stopped going to the gym, and/or avoided good friends.

○ 3. He's moved in with you, or you've moved in with him.

○ 4. Every other time you make a plan with him, he cancels because there's an emergency at home.

○ 5. He continually says you're too sensitive, overreacting, possessive, and so on.

○ 6. He's wondered aloud if maybe he should date other people.

○ 7. You feel lousy about keeping your relationship a secret.

○ 8. You've become obsessed with his wife.

THE DEVIL: YOU THINK HIS WIFE IS THE SOURCE OF ALL EVIL

You already think this. You think it because he thinks it, and you want to bond with him. Right off, you buy into the myth. His wife is a mentally ill person. Furthermore, she is a vengeful witch who is taking his—and your—potential money. The risk is, you come to believe it. You come to believe that this unknown person really does represent everything standing in the way of you and happiness. Remember: It's the rare man who says that he's divorcing a wonderful woman just because he wants a fresh start. A conflict-free divorce is an oxymoron.

So you're pushed into the direction of demonizing her. He comes straight from his lawyer and gives you all the details. You spend every night discussing her latest strategy to make his life miserable. And if he doesn't offer these stories, you feel shut out. You want to know. And what's the other option? If you're not on that side, you have to look at the fact that he has these kids who live in that house with their mother and he doesn't want to give them money.

Granted, it's hard to resist mentally pinning a bull's eye on her forehead. Rachel, thirty-seven, thrilled to hear her not-quite-divorced boyfriend Roger enumerate all the miserable qualities of the woman he was preparing to divorce. "It gave me a sense of security," she says. "I figured, this woman is so awful, their marriage was such a mistake, there's no way the divorce is not going to happen. She made his life hellish. I felt like an angel from heaven next to this woman." Rachel's smugness lasted until the first time she overheard Roger on the phone with the she-devil. "We were at his new apartment, and I'd just come out of the shower and was toweling off, when I hear him engaged in this warm, friendly, intimate conversation with someone. Very soft, very sweet, lots of laughter." In other words, the way he is with Rachel. "I couldn't imagine who it could be. When he got off the phone and said it was her, I was incredulous. It wasn't that he was still in love with her, but it was the first time I really *felt* the history between them. He'd been talking to her like a *husband*. It was a shocker."

Think of his wife as an opportunity for scientific observation. Like a fossil. You get to observe evidence of a romantic life that preceded your own. Yes, it's preserved in a state that's dead. But it's right there, under your nose. It might contain information you can use. "Eddie's wife is very strong, dynamic, organized," says twenty-seven-year-old Alison. Eddie is a painter, Alison a businesswoman. "I can see how Eddie needs a woman with that kind of control to balance out his artistic sensibility. She took care of all the details of their life together." Alison recognizes some aspects of her own personality in Eddie's wife. "Like her, I'm very grounded in reality," she says. "I adore and need Eddie's imagination—it expresses another part of myself. At the same time, I'm aware of the downside of our chemistry because of the way his marriage played itself out. I see how Eddie's wife began to resent his vagueness about things like finances and the kids' schooling. The more she had to take charge of, the tougher and angrier she became— at least, from his point of view. Their chemistry got totally weird. I'm smart enough to see the potential for that in our relationship, and I'm going to do what I can to keep it from hurting us. One difference is that we talk about it. I give him my insights. That's something Eddie and his wife didn't really do."

Joanie, thirty-five, fell in love with Freddie, thirty-seven, a little over a year before his divorce became final. "Freddie told me from the start that his wife had an awful temper, that she was constantly in a rage," she says. "I tried to take it all with a grain of salt, but I felt awful for the guy. He's such a mellow personality, very sweet, and I couldn't imagine how he could have been married for one minute to a woman so unstable. Then, as our relationship evolved, I totally got it. Freddie does this 'poor me' thing, where he feels like the world's on his shoulders—everything just seems to be weighing him down. It's this passivity in him that I see now can drive a person nuts. I don't love him any less, but I understand him—and his first marriage—very well now. I see exactly the role he plays in creating that dynamic. What's different in our marriage is that I see it. And I help him see it."

Why This Devil Is Dangerous

The wife is easy to dismiss when she's the devil incarnate. But understand this: It's not the wife who's a danger to you and your future happiness, it's the nature of divorce itself. If you get sucked into demonizing her—and it's so easy to get sucked in—you get sucked into becoming part of the legal settlement. You think, he's giving her everything! What kind of man is he? How dare she ask for college and camp! He'd better stand up to her! You will have strong feelings, and you will be tempted to express them, to influence him, to possibly radicalize his position—which is an absolute quagmire for your relationship. Divorce is an ambivalent phenomenon in most cases. You will be perceived, ultimately even by him, as having killed his family. If you become overly involved in this transition, in his heart of hearts he will see you as the destroyer. And when he sees his son suffer for his absence or when his daughter's grades go down, you will be the one who caused his children harm.

MEET KENNY
A Man's View (Read It and Weep)

My wife and I hadn't had sex for ten years when I met Suzanne. She was sexy, warm, funny—everything I ever wanted in a woman. I told my wife I wanted a separation and moved out of the house and into Suzanne's. Suzy and I went to Hawaii together and spent the best three weeks of our lives. When we came back, my wife fell apart. She got sick, threatened suicide, the whole deal. I stayed strong and continued to push for a divorce. Meanwhile, Suzy used her money to buy a house, which she assumed we'd live in when we got married. I started to feel kind of trapped. My wife called all the time with reasons for me to come over. The dog is sick. The stereo is broken. Suzy was constantly accusing me of being at her beck and call. I told her it gave us a chance to talk about the divorce, but we did go down memory lane some. I guess the separation actually improved our relationship. Finally, I rented my own apartment and moved out of the house I'd been sharing with Suzy. I can't explain it exactly but I was starting to resent her for being so supportive, for being there no matter what.

That was ten years ago. Suzanne was the love of my life, no question. I don't think I'll ever find another woman more perfect for me. Yet I lost her. We both made some terrible mistakes and killed the relationship. I was so immobilized by guilt back then. I wish Suzy had put her foot down and said, "This is it. I'm gone. Call me when your divorce is final." But she didn't. She thought the best way to help the man she loved was to be understanding, patient, supportive no matter how extreme the situation got.

The bottom line is, I felt I didn't deserve Suzanne's love. I felt like such a bad person for making my ex-wife go through so much pain that I couldn't be loved by anybody. So Suzanne, who gave me the best years of her life, became invisible to me. Never for one second did I stop to think about what she must have been going through. When she asked me about the divorce, I'd say, "Why are you so obsessed about a goddamned piece of paper? You've got me, what more do you want? Can't you see how difficult this is for me?"

Suzanne would say, "It's not the paper, it's the fact that you're still married to another woman." One time Suzanne said something that really hit home. She said, "You don't want to let go of your marriage and the idea of being married to her." And I had to admit she was right.

How to Protect Yourself

Look. Maybe the woman really is a harridan. (Although chances are good that if you were standing next to her in step class, you'd become fast friends.) It's one thing to listen and support, it's another to be drawn into that triangle, to believe his wife's a witch, and to express strong opinions.

He says: "Should I let her have the house? I don't see why I should."

You think: *Let her have it, we'll be done with it.* Or, *What kind of man would let her have the house?*

You say: "I'm sure you'll make the right decision." Or, "Whatever decision you make I'll support you, it's not so crucial one way or the other."

Be cautious. If you begin to lobby, there are going to be repercussions for a long time. You have no business in this negotiation. Your vested interest is not necessarily in the direction of fairness.

The smart move? Appear neutral, reasonable, somewhat disinterested. His divorce is a drama that is happening in his life, not yours. Naturally you're interested in how it's proceeding. You've spoken to him about the time frame; maybe you've spoken to his attorney. You've made your position clear: You have no intention of dating a married man for any significant length of time. Naturally you are interested in how the divorce is affecting his state of mind because you care for him and you have no interest in dating a wreck. You are sympathetic and considerate. At the same time you are confident that he is taking care of business, making good decisions, progressing toward divorce. After all, you are living your rich, full, unpredictable, *single* life as always. If he wants to be a part of it—as you sincerely hope he does—you know that he will do everything possible to make that happen.

Or it's *hasta la vista*, baby.

Save the rage, the tears, the disbelief, and the despair for your best friend, your journal, your therapist, spinning class. If jealousy, anger, and self-pity are a more constant companion than he is right now, get a grip and remember your options:

- You can bail out of the relationship.

- You can put the relationship on hold.

- You can continue with the relationship.

DR. LESLIE PAM'S CHAPTER CHECKPOINTS

1. Is this romance right or wrong? Sometimes your feelings tell you one thing and your mind tells you something different. Your challenge is to balance both. The truth is that both are out there and in there, available to you.

2. Stay in the present. Look and listen. Absorb what he says. He's giving you information all the time—not only what he says, but how he says it; not only what he is, but how he seems.

3. Be brave and bold. Ask tough questions. Follow up on your hunches. Let your unconscious mind process all the information coming your way. Acknowledge the details your conscious mind is gathering, but try to balance what you think with what you feel.

4. If you're feeling needy or desperate, it's a warning that the balance is off. Step back and ask yourself why. He doesn't have that answer—you do. Are you letting the past trip you up? Is he giving you information that you don't want to absorb?

5. You're beginning to form a picture of this relationship. Is this a man you can imagine a future with? Is this a man who sees you as part of his future, or are you his current survival?

CHAPTER THREE

Why Is His Divorce Taking So Long?

W HY IS HIS DIVORCE taking so long? Nothing seems to be happening. He says he loves me, so why aren't we moving forward? Until his divorce is final, we can't make a commitment to a life together. We're excited, we're in love, we're happily compatible in every possible way. So what's the holdup? Why is his divorce taking so long?

It's the drumbeat behind everything else in your life, the one question that haunts your head and heart—even when your love affair itself seems to be going smoothly. Your very existence, your every thought and every conversation—granted, with time-outs for the occasional lovely meal, terrific sex, and the brilliant impersonation you still manage to pull off day after day of a person actually performing a job—has rearranged itself around this question. It makes no difference whether you've been seeing him for three months or three years.

Why is his divorce taking so long?

HOW LONG IS TOO LONG?

Although grounds for divorce (see Appendix A, The Girlfriend's Divorce Primer) and residency requirements differ somewhat from state to state (see Appendix B, A State-by-State Guide to Divorce Laws), most states grant a legal divorce once a couple has lived apart for at least one year.

So the fantasy scenario is that a divorce takes one year.

But the best-case scenario, given that divorces are human enterprises and all human enterprises are essentially flawed, is that a divorce takes between one and two years. Granted, there *are* epic divorces, bitterly contested legal and financial dramas that tie up courts, bank accounts, and the intestinal tracts of the couples involved for years. How do you know if you've walked into one of these nightmares? Remember, by the time you've become lovers, you have made it your business to get straight answers to the following questions:

- When did he move out of the house?

- Do they have a legal separation?

- Have both he and his wife hired lawyers, are they using a divorce mediator, are they trying to settle things themselves?

- Have the papers been served?

- Have they worked out a financial agreement and a child custody agreement?

- Is either one of them contesting the divorce?

- What are his goals in this divorce, and how close is he to meeting them?

Back to the Big Question

Why is his divorce taking so long? When you ask him, he doesn't hesitate to tell you.

Here's his answer: His wife and the lawyers.

This answer appeals to you. It plays to everything you've heard, read, and seen in the movies (remember the black comedy about divorce, *The War of the Roses*?).

Gayle and Elliot, both forty-two, met on an airplane. Each was traveling from New York to Los Angeles on business. It turned out they had mutual acquaintances in the television news industry, were both serious scuba divers, loved Latin food and jazz, and regularly haunted New York's flea markets. Their chemistry was immediate, and they didn't stop talking and laughing the entire flight. Elliot revealed that he had separated from his wife the year before, but wasn't yet divorced. Gayle, who'd had a painful affair with a married man when she was in her early twenties, was wary but game. They met for a drink in L.A., and made plans to get together in New York.

"Elliot had been living a well-established bachelor life for a good year," says Gayle. "He gave off all the signals of an available man. There were no custody issues, just some financial details to work out, which he said they were handling amicably." As Elliot explained it, his lawyer had advised him to hold off signing an agreement until his wife, who was just gearing up to reenter the job market, was earning an independent income. "He wasn't angry with his wife, but he did want to protect his own financial future. It sounded perfectly reasonable," says Gayle. "It's just that, until me, no one had come along to want the process to move more quickly."

When you believe that the progress of the divorce is out of his hands—and in the hands of a professional paid to protect his interests—you can stare lovingly into his eyes over dinner. You mostly hear the part about the two of you having a future together, not to mention one in which by combining your two healthy incomes you get to have the home you always dreamed of.

Elinor, a thirty-three-year-old photographer, fell in love with her mentor, Jack, a forty-six-year-old photojournalist in the middle of a custody fight with his wife over their ten-year-old son. Says Elinor: "My entire life became consumed by his wife's moods. Jack was so torn up by the daily dramas and the fear of possibly losing his kid that I had no problem seeing her as this master puppeteer with our future in her hands. I felt so badly for him."

Yes, divorce is hell. And lawyers and wives are central casting's best picks as the villains of these lower depths. They make sense in this role; they keep you from blaming him, they keep him from blaming himself, and they allow both of you to avoid addressing the real reasons your wonderful love affair has picked up speed but hasn't lifted airborne. If it weren't for the wife and the lawyers, his divorce could proceed and your relationship could move from vague promises about a blurry future to a blissful commitment and a happily-ever-after.

But his wife and the lawyers aren't the real answer to the question haunting your life. On some level you already know this. Otherwise, why would you keep asking the same question?

So why *is* his divorce taking so long? Unless he's lying to you and intentionally malingering (and, as attorney Raoul Felder has already pointed out, some men *do* lie in order to protect themselves from a bad financial settlement and/or further commitment), here's the real answer: Time, and Murphy's Law.

DIVORCE TIME

When you're dating a man getting divorced, you enter another time zone: Divorce Time (DT). DT is battlefield time. Distorted time. Elongated and intensified time. Crisis time. When you live a love affair on DT, your relationship to time itself changes. You actually experience time differently. These are some of the characteristics of Divorce Time:

- Your stress levels are perpetually high.

- You are always On Alert.

- You put more and more energy, thought, and emotion into the relationship.

- You feel more needy.

- You feel emotionally wiped out, like a jet lag that never ends.

At first you assume that what you're feeling is love—that is, the chemical chaos that occurs in the brain when some special stranger causes your endorphins to start slam-dancing and your heart to lurch into the bliss of sexual and spiritual connection. Love is a feeling. In a "normal" love affair, the initial high eventually mellows. (If it didn't, we'd all be skinny, have glowing complexions, and be especially nice to our mothers at all times.) After a few months, feelings organize and channel themselves into a social construction called dating. If all continues to go well, dating evolves to courtship—that is, dating with commitment as a mutual goal. And if two lovers can successfully negotiate the terms of that commitment, their courtship can lead to marriage. In other words, the feelings become part of something bigger—a relationship.

But falling in love is not the same thing as having a relationship. When you are dating a divorcing man, the chemical confusion attendant to falling in love never quite reaches that mellow place. Instead it becomes a low-level, pervasive anxiety that hovers over and around your relationship like soupy grey fog. This feeling is as unsettling as the feeling of falling in love was giddy. You don't like this feeling. You don't want this feeling. This feeling doesn't feel good. It's frustrating, distressing, preoccupying. This feeling isn't love, it's the feeling of a relationship with a great big obstacle in the middle of it. That obstacle is his marital status. So when he tells you that all will be well when his wife and the lawyers settle down, your body isn't buying the story. Your body knows the truth. Your body is on DT, battlefield time, armed to the teeth to defend itself against some unknown enemy.

Here's the good news: You are not really on a battlefield. Your love affair is not really a war. Though you can't control his wife or his lawyer, you can always control your own response to time.

TINA'S STORY

When thirty-five-year-old Tina, a red-haired private-duty nurse with a Julia Roberts smile and a no-nonsense manner, decided to renovate her kitchen, she didn't know she'd get to keep the contractor along with the granite countertop. She fell in love with forty-one-year-old Ben, who showed up in her kitchen only a few weeks after moving out of his own and the twenty-two-year marriage that went with it.

Tina didn't kid herself about the road ahead. "Ben was touchingly, even painfully, sincere with me about everything he was going through right from the start. His marriage was dead, but his guilt and confusion were very much alive—every bit as much as his attraction to me." She resolved to proceed with caution. "I'd never been married before, but my parents divorced when I was eight. I know how much pain and anger and confusion seeps out of a crumbling marriage." Still, as her connection and feelings for Ben deepened, Tina felt a curious disjunction. "Ninety-nine percent of me was certain Ben and I had a future together. He told me he loved me, I felt his love, I loved him back. Our connection felt secure. But that leftover one percent of me freaked out when Ben announced that he and his wife were going into couples therapy, two months after he'd moved out, even though I knew he was doing it to help ease his wife into the divorce process."

Understanding that this unruly one percent of her had the power to create havoc in the way she felt about herself and her life,

Tina took steps to reclaim her own sense of control over events. "I had some time off coming up, so I took a trip to visit friends across the country. That immediately gave me some distance and perspective. When I returned, I made an effort to put myself back into my real life, to see friends and family and regain my equilibrium. It took willpower to take a break from Ben, but I had to do it, to remind myself that I could get nurturing elsewhere in my life." For three weeks Tina continued to speak to Ben, but she didn't see him. "I wasn't trying to manipulate our situation, I was trying to regain myself. I wasn't playing hard to get, I *was* hard to get. I let him know exactly what I was up to."

Tina taught herself a valuable lesson, one she was able to draw on again and again over the next eighteen months. "Every time I put myself first I was able to reassert control. I discovered that I could withdraw from the relationship on good terms and reenter my own separate life. Doing so, I felt my own strength and sanity return. It's not that I learned to love Ben less, but I was reminded that it's a big world out there, that I could find sustenance in it, and that even if Ben and I didn't work out I could find happiness." That feeling is what allowed Tina to reenter Divorce Time renewed, to prevent her frustration from undermining her own sense of worth and her love affair. Less than two years after they met, Ben and Tina married.

Take a Furlough: Revisit Your Own Life

Studies done on soldiers who fought in Vietnam revealed that the men who took furloughs fought less well on their return than those who had remained under battlefield conditions. By returning to "real time" these men went back into the terrible stress of battle with a lowered guard. As a result, they fought less well.

Remember: Love is not really a battlefield, it just feels like one. Your goal is to reduce the stress, because once your crisis is over—when his divorce is final and your relationship no longer exists in an off-kilter world—you don't want the *lack* of tension to undermine your relationship. "Lifeboat" situations—people thrown together under extraordinary circumstances—are famous for deflating when the cause for tension disappears. Soldiers in a battle. Actors on a set. Journalists in a presidential war zone. Pressure throws people together. The energy creates sexual tension. Know that you're meeting under adverse conditions, and these are circumstances that stimulate the romance and the attachment as well as the stress. Stay on good terms with "real time" because the two of you will be living in that time zone down the road.

Renee is a fifty-year-old journalist who was working in London when she fell in love with Peter, a colleague who had taken a temporary assignment in Europe on the heels of a separation from his wife of ten years. "I knew Peter by reputation, knew that he'd just left his marriage," says Renee. "We fell in love quickly and had an idyllic courtship. Then he returned to the States, and I took a job back home soon after, and the divorce battle really heated up. Every day felt like a threat to our happiness together. We were like actors in some terrible soap opera. Finally, eighteen months later, the soap opera was over. There was definitely a period of acclimation, of feeling, "Is this all there is?" Our romance felt flat to me. I was suddenly filled with ambivalence: Do I really want this man? We'd gotten used to being in this battle together. We weren't concentrating on all those mundane relationship issues, like who picks up the milk and who walks the dog and why he's so thinskinned and I'm too quick to lose my temper. We had this whole other reality outside of the two of us to obsess about. Now it was just us. I think that had I been younger I would have thought I was cooling off, that the magic was gone, that I wasn't really in love with this man. We were married a year later, but we definitely had some remedial work to do. We were getting to know each other all over again."

Right now *you* need the skills to get through the battle. Later you'll need the skills to sign the treaty and acclimate to peacetime, when the pressure and the energy it creates no longer exist. You need to know how to do both. You need to take a furlough. You can:

- Renew friendships you've been ignoring.

- Go on a trip.

- Get back to the gym.

- Dedicate new energy to your work.

- Socialize.

- Learn something new: French, pottery, yoga, tap dancing.

- Get a massage.

In other words, reassert control in your own life, care for your body, mine resources you already possess, recharge your energy, reexperience your own charm and appeal. However your love affair turns out, you *must* master the skills and strategies that keep you connected to your own strong self.

From the silver lining department: battlefield conditions test faith. Yes, you've dated a thousand guys and have felt what you now feel for a precious few of them. Yes, this chemistry is rare.

So, will the misery be worth it?

It's your choice. Just because you're having these feelings doesn't necessarily mean he's the guy you're going to spend your life with. It's difficult to give up the feelings. So you have to make it worth it to stay. Finding the balance within yourself between intelligent objectivity and hope will be an ongoing job.

Meanwhile, know this: You've been given an opportunity to grow spiritually, to be in touch with something larger than yourself. On a battlefield, soldiers are pressed to find that bigger reason. Sometimes they do. They find faith. The battlefield of love offers a similar opportunity.

Which will you choose—growth or regression? Take the growth

opportunity and you will be catapulted into a place you'd never have gotten to otherwise, a place you wouldn't have dreamed of volunteering to go—whether he's there with you or not.

How Long Should a Commitment to You Take?

The average courtship lasts between one and two years from meeting to marrying. When did your relationship begin? Some men think that, even if their relationship with you began the day he physically left the marriage, the meter tracking your relationship doesn't turn over until the divorce papers are signed. Wrong. Whatever his reasons for needing or wanting to postpone a commitment to you may be, be confident in your own mind that your relationship with him began when it began. It exists on a separate planet from his divorce. Whether or not you will have it in you to give him more time isn't the point here—either you will find it in yourself, or you won't. Just don't divorce yourself from your own reality.

MURPHY'S LAW

Murphy's Law is the second reason his divorce is taking so long. Murphy's Law says that what can go wrong, will go wrong.

His teenage daughter will develop an eating disorder just before the papers are to be signed, derailing the divorce process and diverting thousands of dollars to a special psychiatric hospital in Sweden.

His wife's father will be arrested for embezzlement, hurling him into a Byzantine subplot (featuring another set of lawyers) for several extra months while he tries to stand by his distraught wife.

His lawyer's plane will be delayed in Aspen, causing him to miss his court appointment for a custody hearing.

PATRICIA'S STORY

I started seeing Max two months after he moved out of the house. With him, it was always, "I'm seeing the attorneys tomorrow . . . everything will be fine . . . it's all underway." There was a lot of money involved, so I should have known better. His wife was the wild card I was always underestimating. She didn't officially know about me, but she must have sniffed it out. Every time Max and I planned an evening or a weekend away, she'd come up with a doozy. Seconds before we were ready to walk out the door, she was calling to plead with him to take the kids because she was going into rehab right that very second to finally deal with her drinking which, needless to say, he had driven her to by leaving and so how could he say no to that, didn't he have to give her a chance, etcetera, etcetera, ad nauseum. Another time we actually made it out of town, had just settled into our hotel room where I was drawing a bubble bath for the two of us when she called hysterical to say that she had developed an infection after liposuction and worried she might have a case of flesh-eating bacteria and the kids were hysterical and she couldn't deal with it. Shut off the water, pack up the suitcase, and all the way back he was trying to explain to me how he just had to be the nice guy or else he'd get screwed in the custody agreement and the settlement. Oh, and when they finally did draw up the custody agreement, she smashed up the car on the way to the attorney's office to sign it.

And so on.

Did you ever remodel your house? Then you know that it took twice as long as promised. Furthermore, when the $20,000 you budgeted was already up to $70,000 and there was a leak and one wall was crooked. . . . Well, you get the picture. Not only does it take twice as long and cost twice as much, you have to figure out how to do damage control every inch of the way. You have to figure out how to live your life and survive the renovation. Assume that his divorce will take twice as long as he estimates and will produce twice as much misery as you think you have it in you to endure. Meanwhile, you will have to figure out how to do damage control, how to live your life, how to survive.

Remember Time and Murphy's Law. You can't do anything about his wife or the lawyers. You can do something about your own response to time. You can't do anything about Murphy's Law but take a deep breath and book a massage.

HOW LONG IS TOO LONG FOR YOU?

Get honest with yourself about your own timetable. You're an individual—not your best friend, not his wife, not even someone you read about in a book. Your timetable is your own. Kathy, forty, met Stephen, fifty, five months after he and his wife had separated. They fell in love and quickly settled into a monogamous relationship. A successful public relations executive, Kathy had been married briefly in her twenties. Though she'd had a few longterm relationships since, none had grown into the kind of commitment she craved. Now all she could hear was the ticking of her biological clock. She was eager to marry and have a child with the right man.

Stephen seemed to have "Mr. Right" scrawled across his forehead. Their friendship, sexual rapport, and compatibility continued to grow. Kathy assumed that Stephen's divorce would come through within another ten months. When six months had passed, they began to talk about "a future together"—meaning, when his divorce was final. She told Stephen that a future for her included a child, that her happiness depended on one. How did he feel about that? He wasn't sure, but he said he was open to the possibility. He just needed to get through the divorce first.

Another four months passed—now, a full year—and still the divorce papers hadn't been signed. Kathy turned forty-one. Her resentment about Stephen's divorce and her anxiety about their future together were spoiling the relationship. Stephen was on good terms with his wife and didn't want to pressure her to move more quickly than was comfortable. He worried that any pressure on his part would jeopardize the financial agreement. Kathy, who hated confrontation, didn't like how angry she was beginning to feel. Did he love her or didn't he? He said he did. When she wasn't feeling angry she was feeling clingy, which she liked even less. She decided to give him an ultimatum: Either he was divorced by the end of the year, or she was moving on. Now Stephen was angry. Why couldn't she be more patient? After all, they were just getting started. And they had such a terrific relationship. And finally, which was more important to her: being with him, or having a child? They spent a painful weekend thrashing round and round the same arguments, not making any headway. Stephen couldn't give Kathy the answer she needed. Kathy couldn't give Stephen more time. Kathy saw it as a choice between loving herself or loving her man. She chose herself. That night they broke up.

What Do You Think of Kathy's Decision?

Maybe your response is "Right on! You go girl!" You're invigorated by Kathy's feisty spirit. You like the fact that she's not settling for leftovers, that she refuses to compromise her dream.

Or maybe you feel: "You blew it, sister. The man is in love with you. Work it a little bit. Use persuasion, not threats. Don't cut off your nose."

In the next chapter, we'll tell you why neither one of those two choices honored the relationship Kathy had established with Stephen. There is a third choice, a choice Kathy wasn't able to see. We'll help you learn to see it. Then we'll help you learn to live it.

In the meantime, you continue to have the same three options you've always had:

- You can bail out of the relationship.

- You can put the relationship on hold.

- You can continue with the relationship.

DR. LESLIE PAM'S CHAPTER CHECKPOINTS

1. There is a phenomenon called "time distortion." When you're having fun, time goes by quickly. Waiting in a doctor's office, a minute can seem like an hour. Each of these emotional states can be defeated by having good information.

2. Continue to develop your information-gathering skills. It's not enough to ask the first question. You must remember to ask follow-up questions, too. Get out a piece of paper, and write down the information that you need and that he gives you.

3. Based on the information he gives you, begin to create your own relationship timeline. As the two of you sit down and negotiate your strategy for being together, you'll begin to see his level of commitment to the relationship.

4. The more committed he is to a plan that includes your thoughts, your ideas, and your timeline, the more flexible you'll find yourself becoming.

5. Now that you have more information, ask yourself: Are your timeline and his on a parallel course, or are you headed for a collision?

CHAPTER FOUR

We're Stuck!
What Do I Do Now?

A T THE BEGINNING OF this book we cautioned you that dating a man getting divorced was risky—so risky that the price could be significant heartbreak, months of your life spent in a relationship leading nowhere, and more months spent recovering from the disappointment. All true. Kathy, who you met in Chapter 3, had had enough of the misery to conclude that she wouldn't be able to stay the course. She decided to cut her losses and bail. Kathy made that choice out of self-knowledge and acted on it. Even though she was convinced it was the right choice at the time, within weeks she regretted it. She loved Stephen and missed him. In her heart she wanted the relationship to work. She wanted to try again. When Kathy called Stephen to suggest it, he was feeling rejected, angry, and skeptical. After all, Kathy had told him time and time again that her heart's desire was a child, and that she didn't think she could be happy without a child. Stephen wasn't prepared to try again. Now he was using her argument against her. Can you blame him?

We believe there's another choice Kathy could have made. It's a choice that you can make, too.

DON'T PLAY IT SAFE, PLAY IT SANE

When a woman falls in love, it quickly becomes evident that there are two ways to handle a relationship crisis: she can play it strategically, or she can go with her feelings.

Most every woman knows how to play by the rules: Don't call him, let him call you; play hard to get; keep him off-balance; give less to get more; and so on. Playing love by the rules works—to a point. Paradoxically, the rules tend to fail us exactly when we need them most—when a relationship hits a snag or is under pressure. That's when we feel most afraid of the loss of love, and that's when our feelings sometimes take over and spoil all our good strategic intentions.

Yet when we give rein to all our "honest" feelings, we often wind up creating just as much misunderstanding. Instead of bringing our lover closer, we drive him further away. Instead of love, clarity, and reciprocity, we feel frustration and disappointment. The reason is that 90 percent of what powers our feelings when we're under stress is the past; namely, all those childhood vulnerabilities and fears. At a time when we need our adult self the most, the child in us runs amuck and takes over. Going with our feelings backfires when our hearts overrun our heads.

We say there's a third choice: Don't play it safe, play it sane. How do you do this?

- You play it sane by focusing on the relationship, not on the goal (his divorce).

- You play it sane by living the relationship day to day, in a manner that allows you to keep your self-esteem and your emotional balance.

- You play it sane by giving up "the rules" and putting your faith in your connection with him. When you play it sane, you don't have to be afraid and you don't have to manipulate.

Will you still feel the pain of disappointment? Yes. Will you still make mistakes? Absolutely. But by keeping your balance day to day, by focusing on the relationship and not the goal (his divorce), you can learn to keep your balance. You can feel the pain without letting it ruin the relationship by turning you defensive. You can choose clarity over confusion. You can make it worth it to stay.

When you play it sane and not safe, you have more influence over his behavior and his heart. You gain authority by being the grown-up in your love affair.

Does playing it sane, not safe, guarantee you a happy outcome? Of course not. But it will give you a sense that today isn't like yesterday and that tomorrow is a brand-new day.

Moreover, when you play it sane, not safe, you stop waiting for happiness to happen, stop waiting for him to deliver perfect love to your doorstep in a great big gift-wrapped box with a card that says "Divorced."

When you play it sane, not safe, you make the choice to be *in* the relationship—right now, with all its imperfections—and not hovering around the edges. You're not a passive audience, you're a participant. You have responsibilities, choices, actions to take. You have control. Your happiness is in *your* hands.

Get busy.

Accept the Limitations

You've drifted from the haze of falling in love into the limbo of waiting for his divorce to happen. Yes, waiting sucks. It's not what you had in mind the first time he kissed you and you felt the world and all its dazzling possibilities open up like a luscious new flower. Not what you had in mind at all. So what *aren't* you getting in the here-and-now of this relationship? Get out a piece of paper and make a list. Be brutally honest with yourself. Maybe the list reads something like this:

What I'm Not Getting Right Now
Being his number one priority
A public social life
Living together
Making plans for the future
A commitment
Having a child together
Spending a whole weekend together without his kids

There you go. Those are the limitations. Can you accept them—not forever and ever but today, right now? More to the point: Can you get the love and nurturing you need today *within* those limitations? Can you design a loving relationship with those limitations as a given? Again, we're not talking about forever. Obviously, you have a limit. (We'll help you figure out if you've reached your limit in Chapter 9.)

Maybe your list will tell you that you've landed in a relationship in which you can't function, in which there's no room to negotiate. Can you live without love and nurturing?

Kathy unintentionally misrepresented her feelings about Stephen and their relationship. Every time the relationship felt stuck, she let the fear control her—that she would miss out on motherhood—rather than assert her own need for commitment, love and nurturing. Rather than accept the limits in the relationship *for now*, she panicked. And she drove Stephen away.

We think Kathy had a better choice, one that honored her true feelings. She could have said to Stephen: "The most important thing to me is being in a relationship with you. I'd love to have a child and I'm hoping we will, but either way I want to be with you. I just want to know if you have the ability to commit to me and be in this relationship as deeply as I am and as I want you to be." If she had said this, she would have shown an acceptance of the limitations in the present moment.

Replace Expectations with Obligations

"If he loved me, he'd *want* to make the divorce happen." Margo, thirty-two, is chanting this all-too-familiar refrain to herself. She is truly stymied. This refrain makes as much sense in her own head as B follows A. Margo and Graham have been involved for a year and a half. He adores her, tells her all the time how she's changed his life, lit up the darkness, infused his days with meaning. But Graham's divorce is moving at glacial speed. He's dragging his feet, waffling about the financial settlement, throwing out one excuse after another to justify the leisurely pace of the legal process. Margo offers Graham different versions of this refrain: "If you loved me, you'd introduce me to your kids. If you loved me, you'd tell your wife that you met someone and need to get on with your life. If you loved me, you'd tell the kids they can't stay over during the week. If you loved me, you'd give me a timeline."

Margo's "If you loved me . . ." conversation gets her nowhere, except back to the self-pity of deprivation and the resentment that comes from passively waiting for something she wants and can't have. Worse, it has no effect on Graham except to leave him irritated and annoyed, wearing a baffled look on his face.

Are you all too familiar with "If he loved me he'd . . ."? Don't go there. There *is* no there there.

Instead, get active. You take charge of establishing ground rules for the *actual, limited* relationship the two of you have now.

Consider the first limitation on our suggested list: you're not his number one priority. What is? His number one priority is navigating his divorce—with all the emotional, legal, and financial pressures that implies—and remaining intact. His first priority is survival, his own psychic and financial survival in the wake of a life, of a chunk of his own history, unraveling. Yes, you represent pleasure, a resting place, and an enjoyable diversion from that ordeal, even the hopeful promise of a new future. But if you think that right now, today, he will choose pleasure over survival, you're deceiving yourself. He will choose survival over pleasure every time. He has to. He has no choice. You would, too.

So delete "If you loved me you'd . . ." from your handbook of divorce phrases. Don't say it to him, and don't say it to yourself.

Instead, replace it with: "I don't need to be your number one priority, but I do need to be more than an afterthought in your life. I can't be satisfied with leftovers." Write this down. Tape it to your bathroom mirror. Practice saying it aloud to yourself for a few days. When it starts to feel like a part of you, say it to him. Explain to him, sweetly and emphatically, that in order to get the nurturing from you that he so adores, he has to nurture you in return. After all, that's why the two of you are in this relationship. It's the fundamental bottom-line contract between both of you. Reassure him that for the time being you've accepted the limitations, and given up your expectations. You're a reasonable person, and a loving one. You'd like to give what you can in spite of the limitations that exist today. Now it's his turn. He has an obligation, too. It's his responsibility to give what he can in spite of the limitations.

While you're at it, tape this to the mirror as well: *No matter what, he has to give to me.*

Be Unafraid to Actively Negotiate

Do you think it's unromantic to negotiate the nitty-gritty terms of your relationship? Maybe you're afraid that when you put what you want in actual words—that you'd like to hear from him at least once a day or that you want him to give you advance warning about which weekends he'll be spending with his kids—you'll sound unreasonable and demanding, even if what you want is reasonable and easily given. If it can't be given, wouldn't you rather face that now than two years down the road? What do you need? What do you want? What does he have it in him to give? Factor in the limitations that exist today, figure out what's reasonable, and ask for it.

Caroline, thirty-eight, wanted a timeline and regular updates. She met Bradley, forty, at a dinner party given by mutual friends. Caroline had heard about Bradley for years, knew the story of his wife's affair with a colleague, that his wife had wanted the divorce, that they'd been living apart now for several months, that the emotional chaos around the way the marriage had ended was beginning to settle down. Friends thought Caroline and Bradley would hit it off, and they did. They fell in love. Bradley walked her home from that dinner party, Caroline invited him in, and that was that. Eight months later, that was still that. Bradley's divorce, which he had assured her that very first night was "a signature away," had hit a snag. Bradley's wife and the man with whom she'd had the affair had broken up. She didn't want Bradley back, but the pressure on her end to obtain a divorce had let up. "I figured she was ambivalent," Caroline explains. "She was comfortable with the financial terms of the separation, so she was in no hurry to sign the papers. Bradley was comfortable, too. They'd reached this resting place, where further and possibly painful or confrontational action didn't seem to be necessary." They'd have stayed there were it not for the existence of Caroline. "Although I felt pretty certain that Bradley would never go back to the marriage and was secure about our relationship, I worried that the shift in circumstances had to make him somewhat ambivalent, too."

Caroline had been telling Bradley all along that dating a married man was not what she had in mind and warned him that she wasn't going to wait forever. For one two-week period, they'd taken a break, not seen or spoken to each other at all. Now she told Bradley that she needed to know what his *specific* plan was to move the divorce along. He waffled, rationalized, then simply confessed to feeling stuck. He wondered if maybe he needed some time on his own. Maybe he was still too angry at his wife to fully commit to Caroline. Caroline chose not to panic. "I was worried, but grateful that he could say all this to me. He didn't shut me out." Caroline was sympathetic, but firm. "I told him that I definitely couldn't continue without a timeline and a plan. But I gave him one out. If he couldn't come up with one now, would he consider entering therapy together to air some of the reasons why he couldn't."

Bradley mulled over Caroline's idea for a week, then agreed to see a therapist with her for a limited number of sessions. At the end of four sessions, Bradley was able to formulate a plan to move the divorce forward. He'd taken control. Caroline was satisfied. "By seeing the therapist in the first place I could see that he was seriously committed to our relationship, and she really did help him figure out how to deal more effectively with his wife." Six months later, the divorce papers were signed. Caroline and Bradley are making plans to marry.

The moral of the story: negotiate for the rights you need along the way.

If he won't negotiate and refuses to give you the right to say what's on your mind, think very seriously about taking a break or ending the relationship. If he doesn't want to hear your observations, you're probably saying something he's afraid to hear. Eventually, he has to be willing to hear what you have to say. Otherwise, the two of you are well on your way to establishing a dysfunctional relationship. If the flow of conversation stops or is restricted by too many rules, the relationship dies.

Don't play Melanie to his wife's Scarlett

Do you remember Melanie and Scarlett in *Gone with the Wind*? Melanie was good, wise, all-giving, all-understanding. Scarlett had all the fun. Naturally, most of us want to be Scarlett. It's the classic good girl/bad girl split. But in the drama of divorce, the wife is always cast as the bad woman. That leaves the good woman role for you, and you may take it all too willingly. Why? Because a funny thing happens when we're under pressure. We assume roles we'd never consider taking on otherwise. If she's going to be demanding, unstable, unpredictable, and horrific, you fully intend to be your most patient, supportive, absorbent, and eternally flexible sweet self. There's just one problem with this setup. Him. He didn't fall in love with Melanie the good woman, he fell in love with you. By playing the good woman all the time, not saying what's on your mind, being everything to him that she isn't, you make it impossible for him to let go of the bad woman.

So be your actual cranky, demanding self. Insist on being that self. Speak from your instincts and your heart. If necessary, tell him: "You know, I find myself in a situation where it's hard to be real. I don't want to be any of the things you don't like, but I'm a human being. I need to be more myself." He's likely to say: "Gee, I want you to be more yourself." Forget about being like her or not like her.

Recognize the difference between being real and being needy. When you're real, you allow your faith in the good of the relationship to guide you. When you're needy, you allow your fears and insecurities to control you.

Lucy, thirty-one, and thirty-four-year-old Glenn knew each other for several years as work colleagues and friends before Glenn and his wife separated. By then Lucy had heard all the war stories about Glenn's marriage. Although she was sympathetic to Glenn—his wife sounded unstable and, after he asked for the divorce, vindictive—she felt free as a friend to share her observations about Glenn's behavior as well. There was always an attraction between Lucy and Glenn, but it didn't blossom until Glenn had moved out. By then Lucy had moved on to another job. "I was so accustomed to hearing these horror stories about Glenn's wife. As his friend, I was kind of feisty and disapproving of her and encouraged him to stand his ground. It was part of why he fell in love with me. But the minute we became lovers and were involved romantically, the last thing I wanted to do to Glenn was put pressure on him. He already had that aggravation in his life."

Lucy tried to swallow her impatience and resentment as the divorce dragged on. If she had a complaint, she took it to a friend. "I got sick of hearing about his wife. I was angry at Glenn for being a pushover and for continuing to treat me as this infinitely absorbent sponge. I mean, was I the woman he loved or wasn't I?"

By trying to keep her relationship with Glenn free of stress, Lucy only succeeded in keeping it free of Lucy. Instead of presenting Glenn with her loving, supportive, cranky, demanding, complicated self—the woman he'd fallen in love with—she offered him Melanie, the good woman. But Glenn didn't fall in love with Melanie, he fell in love with Lucy. And by giving him only part of herself, she was depriving the relationship of the intimacy it needed to thrive.

Don't play it safe. Don't be afraid to be cranky when you feel cranky. It's okay to say, "Listen, buddy, I'm not your princess savior. I'm willing to give back as long as you're giving. I refuse to be everything your wife isn't. In fact, maybe I'll be just as demanding and impossible. But whatever happens, I'm going to be myself. I need to be myself."

Again, distinguish between being real and being needy. Being real means being honest, which can be scary—it means setting limits, letting him know what feels good to you and what doesn't, and risking losing him. Being needy means twisting yourself into pretzels for the relationship, calling him too many times a day because you haven't embraced your own life, swallowing your anger in order to sweetly seduce more attention out of him, and tugging at him for reassurance.

Don't play it safe. Under battlefield conditions the good commanding officer says, "Forget the bullets for the moment. If we don't get food and water for the troops we're going to starve to death here." You are in a relationship under siege. The pressure will force you to be more real than you're comfortable being. Resist the temptation to retreat. Refuse to pretend.

Lucy and Glenn decided to put their relationship on hold until Glenn's divorce was final. Lucy began to date again. When Glenn came back to her a year later, divorced, she had met someone new and was involved. That relationship ultimately ended. Lucy and Glenn are dating.

Use Strategy When Necessary

We told you that games and manipulation don't get you where you want to be—in a loving and nurturing relationship—and we stand by that. Games, manipulation, and rules might be acceptable dating tactics, but dating is lower on the romantic food chain than where you are now—in a battlefield relationship with a man you love who is getting divorced.

Strategy is the thinking woman's battlefield defense.

Kim is a thirty-five-year-old actress who was in the winding-down phase of a troubled relationship when she met fifty-year-old Steve, a hedge fund manager, on a blind date. Steve was in the fourth year of pursuing his divorce after a fifteen-year marriage. He'd been out of the house for three years, but was taking his time, dating, spending time with his kids, hanging on to his money. Kim and Steve were crazy about each other, but Kim was wary. When Steve called her the day after their first dinner date to make another plan, Kim was straight with him. "I think you're great," she told him, "but I'm still involved and, even if I weren't, I could never consider you in a serious way because you're not divorced." Steve left town shortly after that for an extended business trip, but he continued to woo Kim with phone calls and flowers. While he was away, Kim's other relationship sputtered to a close. When Steve returned, she accepted another date with him, and they began seeing each other regularly.

Kim's position hadn't changed; until Steve was divorced, she wouldn't accept him as a serious suitor. Was Kim crazy about Steve? Yes. But she had managed to subtly establish the relationship on *her* terms from the get-go: She was the prize, a woman worth winning. Until he could offer her what she wanted in a serious romance—a commitment—she wouldn't take the relationship seriously. Kim's strategy was instinctive. It reflected her self-worth, her ability to put her love for herself before her feelings for Steve. Her attitude was sweet but firm: *You're a nice guy,* it communicated, *but what's in it for me?*

Steve had dated a lot of women since he moved out of the house he'd shared with his wife. He was successful, attractive, and wealthy. An army of women had already fallen in love with Steve since his separation; their corpses still littered his address book. But he'd never met a woman who—aside from being sexy, charming, and sweet—was secure enough to treat him as, well, an applicant. Kim was irresistible. Self-love established the ground rules for her relationship with Steve, but strategy enforced the rules. She kept her other romantic options open. She didn't allow herself to get too comfortable in Steve's life. Sometimes when he called she didn't answer the phone. If she was in a bad mood, she didn't see him. When she felt especially frustrated or needy, she took her complaints to her girlfriends. This is not to say she wasn't real with Steve. Her reality was: If you want me, get moving.

After a month, Kim's ex came back into her life, hoping to try again. Kim decided to give him another chance. When she told Steve, he was devastated. He told her he loved her and that the divorce would happen any day now. The holiday season was coming up, and he wanted Kim to take a trip and meet his kids. Kim knew in her heart that she and her ex weren't going to make it. Nevertheless, she turned Steve down, saying she planned to spend the holidays with him. This was tough on Kim. Steve was the man she wanted. But she knew the holidays without her would be tough on Steve, and she saw it as a test. Her strategy paid off. By Valentine's Day, Steve's divorce papers were signed and Kim found an engagement ring in her tiramisu—in Venice.

Use Language to Say What You Mean and Get What You Want

That sounds pretty obvious, right? Why else do we use language? Furthermore, everyone knows that women are professional talkers, especially good at parsing every emotion known to humankind, highly trained in the arts of subtext, nuance, subtlety, and persuasion—right? Well, not necessarily. Think back to Kathy, whose anxiety that she might miss out on motherhood drove away the one man she wanted to share that experience with. We don't always get what we want because we don't always say what we mean.

Psychologists say it takes a person about five times to say what he or she really means in a conversation. Consider the first time you open your mouth as a kind of rough draft. You have to keep editing, adding to, and tweaking your communication until you're confident it's really getting your meaning across. It helps if your partner is sufficiently motivated to help you edit and refine by continually asking, "What do you mean?" But when the stress is on, it's hard to be clear and just as hard to helpfully edit.

Practice on a girlfriend. Try out what you need to say to him with her first. Teach your friend to keep asking you, "Is this what you mean?" and to repeat it back until you can truly say, "Yes, that's what I mean."

SOME PRINCIPLES OF COMMUNICATION
Use Action Statements; "I" Instead of "You" Statements

Bad Choices

"If you really loved me, you'd push harder for the divorce."

"You have no backbone. Can't you see she's jerking you around?"

"You're taking advantage of me, manipulating my feelings for you."

Better Choices

"I'm not good at waiting. I want to be involved in a relationship that has a timeline."

"Although you're doing the work, I'd like to know how I can help. And I need an update."

"I need to say that things are moving too slowly."

"I'd like your permission to be the strong one when you're waffling. I'd like to divide up the duties, to offer you my strength and support. I want the right to say what's on my mind, even if I risk chasing you away."

"I'm a valuable commodity, but I'm like water in your hands. I can't be with you if you won't squeeze your hands together as hard as possible. I'll know you see me as valuable if you come up with a specific plan."

What You Need to Hear from Him

At best, a real and specific plan. Short of a plan, a willingness to engage in the conversation with you, and a positive response to your opinions. Get to know the difference between conversation and excuse.

Let Yourself Make Mistakes

Get it through your head that it's okay to "blow it" every now and then, that it would be terrifically weird if you didn't occasionally screw up and say or do the "wrong" thing. The point is, you're in a relationship, not trying out for the Navy Seals. There's little you can do that's irrevocable. But you must stay aware of what serves your sanity and what doesn't—*your* sanity comes first and foremost, not his. If you're fearful that the occasional screw-up with him will result in bigtime penalties—like his immediately returning to his wife—you might want to think about who is setting the standard here, you or him. If it's him and not you being too hard on yourself, you're in the wrong relationship. There's nothing loving about walking on eggshells.

You may make mistakes when you're frustrated, and you may become frustrated when you try to overcome an obstacle by doing the same thing over and over with zero results. Let's say you've had the "Where are we?" conversation five times and still there's no movement in the divorce. Now you're just fighting with him, using all those forbidden "you" zingers intended to vaporize him with blame.

You need to take a break. Take a step backwards. Right now it's important that you deal with your frustration, not his divorce.

How big a step back do you need to take? Some women throw themselves into work, friends, exercise, or extra sessions with their therapist; others date; and there are women who simply step back only as far as the bedroom door, deciding to discontinue a sexual relationship until he can make a commitment to their relationship. Your step back will reflect whatever it takes for you to feel centered in your own life again. There's no faking it, either. That's the difference between strategy and manipulation. Strategy takes the long view: What will serve *me*? not, What will change *him*? And what serves you is whatever returns you solidly to yourself, puts you back in control of your own life, and safeguards your sanity. Remember: It doesn't matter what course your journey takes as long as you get where you want to go. You always have three options:

● You can bail out of the relationship.

● You can put the relationship on hold.

● You can continue with the relationship.

DR. LESLIE PAM'S CHAPTER CHECKPOINTS

1. Don't be willing to stay stuck. Let him know if you object to how things are going between you. Tell him that even though it's not a problem—yet—at some point in the future it will become a problem if you don't deal with it.

2. Suggest that the two of you sit down and come up with a plan together. Tell him, "I'm willing to do anything and everything possible to make this happen."

3. The man who insists on doing it all himself is not the partner you've been looking for. If he's excluding you from the solution, he doesn't see you as part of the future.

4. The man who is willing to sit down with you and formulate a plan that makes sense is the kind of man you're looking for—even if that means he needs some time alone to take care of certain elements of his divorce. If he needs time alone, give it to him.

5. Listen for the man who says: "I know that you are a resource for me. I know that you've been extremely patient. I know that I'm not giving you what you need right now." Being stuck is a real test of his ability to be aware of you, to not be completely obsessed with his own life.

CHAPTER FIVE

Anatomy of the Divorcing Male

HOW TO TELL A LOSER FROM A KEEPER

ALL DIVORCING MEN ARE not created equal.

Some are diamonds-in-the-rough, perfectly good guys and potential husband material temporarily immobilized in full-body emotional casts, sweet hunks of burning love licking their wounds and waiting to be recycled into the hotblooded arms of the next worthy woman (you).

Others are defective. They are losers of various stripes—husbandly nightmares temporarily disguised as eligibile men in suits, dating Houdinis destined to slip from your embrace somewhere between the separation agreement and the final court date, commitmentphobes who some hopeful woman once hauled into marriage and has now heaved out, serial marriers and divorcing bachelors-for-life content to date you while keeping one eye peeled for the next babe or the nearest exit, whichever comes first. Really. After all, how hard is it for a man—any man—to get married?

But there's third group: Men who can be transformed from losers to keepers.

Your challenge is to learn how to separate the losers from the keepers, how to recognize the loser who can be transformed into a keeper, and—trickiest of all—how to keep yourself from turning a keeper into a loser.

This chapter will tell you how.

How to Spot a Loser

Divorcing men with the following identifying characteristics aren't necessarily emotional miscreants or even nightmare romantic prospects for perpetuity. Like your averagely flawed single man, these men might well fulfill their commitment potential one or two relationships from now. Are you willing to risk being his transitional relationship? If so, you *can* turn some of these men into keepers. But better roll up your sleeves: Your work is cut out for you.

He hasn't filed and has no plans to. What you're tempted to think: *Well, he's moved out and he says that the marriage is definitely over. There must be financial details to work out. I'll wait and see.*

How you should respond: "Call me when your divorce is underway or a done deal. I'll look forward to dating you then." Ask yourself how long you're willing to wait because, basically, you're dating a married man. He just happens to be living apart from his wife and family, waiting for who knows what: to work things out, to win the lottery, for his wife to change her mind, etc. It's hard to say, and that's the point. You don't want to be guessing.

Does he have keeper potential? Not until, at the very least, he files the papers. If your relationship started before he moved out, you may very well be seeing this as a giant step forward. Get a grip on yourself. This is far from a done deal. Even if you don't break it off entirely, this isn't a moment to take a deep breath filled with relief. Moving out was probably traumatic enough for him. Expect the other side of the ambivalence to kick in—not only regret and guilt about the marriage, but uncertainty about your waiting arms. Rein in your impulse to jump for joy. You've still got a long road ahead of you.

He doesn't have a clue what went wrong in his marriage. What you're tempted to think: Taking his words—his marriage went sexually stale, his wife and he grew apart, he married too young, his wife had an affair—at face value. Okay, maybe he even takes blanket responsibility, as in he had an affair or he poured too much of himself into his work or she was just too damn good for him from the get-go. Each of these stories makes appealing dramatic sense to you. You recognize these stories; they're familiar. What's more, told from the point of view of the hapless victim or an equally hapless bad boy—him—the lessons in the story leave an appealing role for you to fill: you get to be the enchanting heroine riding to his rescue, ready to be his soulmate.

How you should respond: Men who give boilerplate explanations (excuses) for the end of a marriage or who dump their equally unreflective guilt into your lap are either not giving you their full attention and/or are destined to enter a rebound relationship and make all the same mistakes again. You don't want to be that rebound relationship, and you certainly want to be taken seriously enough to hear the real story.

Be skeptical when a man offers zero insights about what went wrong in his marriage. That doesn't mean he has to have it all figured out, just that he has to acknowledge some responsibility over the failure and has to be willing to share those thoughts with you. Confusion over what went wrong is a more promising psychic state than blanket blame or guilt.

Ask him what *he* did wrong in his marriage. If he's not interested enough to take the trouble to tell you, forget him. If he just can't come up with anything remotely resembling personal responsibility, spoon-feed him some encouragement. Tell him you've discovered the opposite in your own relationships, that it's natural to want to see yourself in the best possible light after a failure but that the responsibility always belongs to both partners and it's helpful to distinguish the "me" problems from the "we" problems. Does he still have that "Huh?" look on his face? If he refuses to buy the premise, throw him back.

Does he have keeper potential? Yes, if he's open to what you have to say, if he's willing to think about what went wrong in his marriage, if he's in therapy or open to the idea of therapy, if you see that he is actively trying to make sense of his romantic history, if he can say at the very least that though he doesn't know what mistakes he made, he certainly doesn't want to make them again.

He falls in love with you on the first date. How you're tempted to respond: The way any woman would—by feeling flattered, if skeptical. Even if you haven't made up your own heart, you're willing to be won over by his ardor. You're not an idiot. You're protecting yourself with the basic dating-savvy, wait-and-see attitude any sane woman has. But surrendering to his all-out pursuit—by falling in love, embarking on a sexual relationship, responding to his ardor in kind—can lead to a messier heartbreak than when you fall for his single-guy double. When the fireworks fizzle a bit (and they always do), the divorcing man leaves a particularly miserable morning-after—like, his actual divorce. It keeps you hanging in, blaming *it* and not *him* for all the problems. It's more appealing to see the relationship obstacle as outside of him in the form of his still-pending divorce than inside of him, as in his fear of getting close again.

How you should respond: Go ahead and let him become smitten, but devise a few speed bumps to slow him down! Be the one who sets the romantic pace. Make a deal with yourself—you can let him in on it, too—that you won't consider any avowals of undying love or growing old together as on-the-record genuine until his divorce itself is official and the playing field between you becomes level. Remember the faux-marriage trap—this is a man who knows how to get intimately involved *fast*. What's more, he's looking for emotional CPR. Yes, you're developing a relationship, deepening your intimacy, and taking to heart his commitment to the here-and-now of your romance. Just don't focus on tomorrow. He isn't. Basically, the here-and-now is all you have. Put your money on how giving and available he is to you day to day, how open if cautious he is about an eventual future, *not* on vague promises about that eventual future. Remember, he can afford to come flying toward you at warp speed with vague promises—he's completely unfree to back them up.

Does he have keeper potential? Maybe, but there are few guarantees. After a dead marriage, a brand-new love affair is ecstatically invigorating to a man and impossible to resist. Robert, a fifty-year-old surgeon who had been married sixteen years to "the wrong woman," fell for Daisy one month before his final divorce papers were signed. "My wife was a very difficult woman," he says. "Daisy was light and airy and sexy and fun. We had wonderful times together. She was exactly what I needed at the time." Robert's "at the time" lasted close to five years. He wound up marrying a woman he met toward the end of his relationship with Daisy. So what made her the transitional woman? "My theory is that people tend to marry the parent they had the most emotional difficulties with, in an attempt to solve those problems," says Robert. "My first wife was a lot like my mother—difficult and controlling." His second wife is cut from the same cloth, he says, "but she's a much improved version!" Robert adds that he "knew it wasn't going to last" with Daisy. "She was great company, but she didn't have the same social or intellectual background as I have, and she was a different religion." Are you congratulating yourself for being everything his wife isn't? Think it over.

He hasn't moved out of the house. What you're tempted to think: *It's poor timing, but a mere detail. After all, the divorce is something they've both agreed to. I'm lucky I met him before he* *started dating for real.*

How you should respond: If you're dating a man who shares a roof with his wife, you're having an affair with a married man. Is that how you want to see yourself? We didn't think so. This one's a no-brainer. If he hasn't moved out—even if he's sleeping in another room or living in the basement like a mole person—this couple is emotionally embroiled. Physical separation is such a giant psychological step that the courts have gone to the trouble of legalizing it as a divorce prerequisite. When two people are still sharing the same address, they haven't done the emotional work necessary to begin that process. This is a triangle with *really* sharp edges. Stay clear.

Catherine, a thirty-five-year-old advertising copywriter, fell in love with Joe, an attorney, when the two met in a screenwriting class. "I dated Joe several times—he told me he was at the tail end of his divorce—before we slept together, at his place," says Catherine. That was when Catherine discovered that Joe's wife Marla's clothes (size 6) still filled the closets. Marla's shampoo and conditioner occupied a corner of the bathtub. Marla, who had asked for the divorce, was in another country with her lover. Catherine and Joe continued to see each other, seemingly in love, right through the final papers. But it didn't really matter. The real story was in those closets, in that bathroom. "I came to realize that Joe was still hopelessly enmeshed with Marla," Catherine says. "He'd gone along with the divorce like a good boy, hoping she would have the fling and come back to him." Eventually Marla did come back—to pack up her belongings for good. By that time, Joe was in an immobilizing depression and his romance with Catherine had crashed and burned. "I really got my heart smashed to smithereens," says Catherine.

Does he have keeper potential? Not this round. Make a graceful exit and let him know you'd love to pick things up again when he's free. If you take a walk now, chances are good he'll be back—and, if you're lucky, divorced!

He speaks to and about his wife disrespectfully. What you're tempted to think: *The bitch! Thank goodness I'm nothing like that piece of work.*

How you should respond: "I wonder if the day will come when he speaks to me exactly the same way." The best predictor of future behavior is past behavior. Men are broadcasting crucial information about their values all the time. How he treats the people he's closest to (and that includes his own mother and other family members) is a powerful indicator of how he'll treat you. Yes, divorce is human nature *in extremis*. We say ugly hateful things when we're angry and hurting. It's your job to determine whether disrespectful behavior is just temper and temporary or a more deeply ingrained aspect of his character. Are you willing to absorb this information?

"I was lying in bed with Kenny one morning when he took a call from his wife," says thirty-seven-year-old Jessie. "We'd been seeing each other for about a month, and I thought I'd never met a sweeter man. That morning I heard a coldness and a sarcasm come out of him that really alarmed me. I don't even think he was aware that there was anything wrong with the way he spoke to her. When we had our first argument a few weeks later—about a man at a party he thought I was paying too much attention to—I heard that same tone of voice and saw him turn on me. I came to know that tone of voice as who he was when he felt hurt and angry and defensive. It was an intractable part of him, that defensiveness, and I think we fell apart because of it. But I first heard it when he spoke to his wife on the phone that morning."

Does he have keeper potential? Keep your ears open. Play devil's advocate: "There must be something lovable about your wife. What was it about her that made you fall in love in the first place?" Tell him that his disrespect concerns you. Find out why she makes him so mad. At the very least, suggest that he keep his battles private. Draw a few lines and see if he respects them. We're not suggesting you become his wife's one-woman fan club, just that you check out whether his hostility and anger level is situational or constitutional.

He worries that he's not being "fair" to you and/or encourages you to date others. What you're tempted to think: *He's a good guy who respects me, is aware of his semi-availability, and wants to do the right thing. Anyway, it doesn't matter what he says. He's here isn't he?*

What you should think: *The man wants his freedom.* It might be too early in your romance to have a where-is-this-going conversation, but if you've been seeing each other for some months and are sexually intimate, his actively encouraging you to keep your options open is a sign that he's not taking your relationship as seriously as you are. We like a divorcing man who thinks of *you* as the gatekeeper to increasing sexual and emotional intimacy. He's the one with all the baggage—he should be counting his lucky stars he's involved with you at all. If he's concerned about how "fair" he's being, understand that he is eager to secure the most possible freedom for himself without feeling guilty.

Does he have keeper potential? He might, but only if you're willing to take him at his word. Lower your investment in this relationship *right now*. Keep your heart open for other men. Don't just wait for him to see the light. He's sending you a message. Actively pursue other dating options.

He's secretive about his life apart from you. What you're tempted to think: *I don't need to hear the blow-by-blow of his divorce and his problems with his kids and what he did between two and four on Sunday afternoon. He's discreet—he doesn't want to burden our romance with too much information. He's busy—now that there's more finanical pressure on him, he has to work twice as hard. He's cautious—that's reasonable after the breakup of a marriage.*

How you should respond: If you've been dating him more than a few months, are sexually intimate, and either he's not talking about or not sharing other parts of his life with you, start wondering why this minute. Ask: Are you dating other women? Do you think I'm not interested in these other parts of your life? If you notice a change in his willingness to include you or an unavailability that wasn't there before, pay attention.

Ginger, a forty-one-year-old medical technician, met Alan, thirty-five, just after she separated from her husband of twenty years. Alan was also recently separated, the father of a four-year-old daughter. "There was an instant attraction, and we immediately started commiserating over our divorces," says Ginger. During the first year of a wonderful love affair, Ginger got her divorce. Alan's wife was still fighting him over custody of their daughter. "Still, we were in love—it was incredible between us. Great sex, lots of affection and intimacy. I was crazy about his daughter, and she adored me. We talked a lot about our future together." Sometime during the second year of their relationship, there was a subtle shift. "Alan seemed busier than usual. Where he used to see me every day or every other day, suddenly he had more work responsibilities. But he was still loving on the phone, the sex was still great, we still talked about the future." It took Alan two-and-a-half years to settle his divorce. "It came through on a Friday. That weekend he was out of town. He came back on Monday and called me. He'd gotten married over the weekend to a woman he'd been seeing for six months." Ginger was flattened, to say the least. "Looking back, I can see the change in him. I was the one making all the effort in the relationship. He was definitely pulling back." And, of course, lying.

Does he have keeper potential? Only if you downsize your emotional investment in the relationship to equal his or withdraw until he can offer you more. What's not going to work is badgering him to share more of himself. Disengage to whatever extent it takes to feel better about yourself, and take your focus off what you're *not* getting.

You can't tell him what you think about his divorce. What you're tempted to think: *His divorce is a sensitive subject, and it's natural for him to be defensive. Anyway, it wasn't my marriage so I should stay out of it.*

What you should think: *If we are more than casually dating and I don't have his permission to express what I think or observe with-*

*out blaming or attacking or criticizing, I'm not in an intimate rela-
tionship. Why doesn't he want to hear what I have to say? Is he
afraid? What's he afraid of?*

Does he have keeper potential? Not as long as you can't tell him
what you think and he isn't offering you any good explanation or
insight into his resistance; *i.e.*, he cares for you but isn't ready to
discuss the blow-by-blow of his divorce settlement with you or he
hears your observations about how his kids walk all over him as
criticism. Throw him back if he shuts you down.

He hasn't established clear boundaries with his wife and his kids.
What you're tempted to think: *He feels so guilty about the divorce,
he can't take a stand. This will stop once the divorce is farther along,
and the kids stop acting out, and his wife has met someone else.*

How you should respond: His emotional attachment to the
marriage—even if that attachment seems to be a negative one
born of guilt or anger—is undermining his desire to be with you.
If he can't set limits around his availability and preserve those limits, if he routinely makes promises to you then breaks them, your
relationship is probably doomed for now. We're not suggesting
that he should be limiting his availability to his kids—in the next
chapter we'll be discussing this at greater length—just that you
can't consistently be getting the leftovers. If you are and find yourself always swallowing your resentment, you'd be wise to take a
giant step back.

Does he have keeper potential? Not the way things stand now.
If he can't make you more of a priority, make him less of one.

He has a pattern of infidelity. What you're tempted to think:
That was then, this is now.

How you should respond: If infidelity was a constant all through
his marriage, it's in your interest to discover why. More to the
point, does *he* know why? Some men with big-time commitment
issues simply manage their anxiety by never fully committing, even
to a marriage. Or is there an element of sexual compulsion in his

romantic history? Exercise due diligence. You wouldn't buy a house without a thorough inspection. If there are cracks in his foundation, *caveat emptor!*

Does he have keeper potential? Maybe, if he owns up to the pattern and is willing to consider therapy. But for you, right now? What would you tell your best friend if she came to you with a similar story?

How to Spot (and Keep) a Keeper

Sometimes only one crucial thing stands between a loser and a keeper: You. The keeper isn't made of dramatically different DNA than the loser. He didn't necessarily have a happier childhood or a less hideous marital failure or watch more Oprah or have intensive psychotherapy. He's just less stuck in some love-challenged place. Maybe he's further along in the divorce process than when you first met him. Or he's more ready for the hopeful changes a new love brings. For any one of a thousand reasons, he's more responsive to *your* influence. Your challenge is to exercise that influence wisely. Any one of these keepers could go bad with a little effort on your part. Don't turn a keeper into a loser.

He isn't sure he wants to marry again. What you could think: *Oh, great! At heart he's just your basic commitmentphobe. Why would I want to continue a relationship with a man who doesn't see marriage as a goal? Does he think I'm dating for the sheer pleasure of it? Does he assume I'm investing time and emotional energy in a not-yet-divorced man for research purposes? Who does he think he is, anyway?*

How you should respond: Get off your high horse. A not-quite-divorced man who feels cynical or just uncertain about remarriage is coming at you from a more honest place than a divorcing man who is promising you the moon on the second date. After all, he's suffered a major life disappointment. Why wouldn't he feel skeptical?

"This is the first time in my life I've been without direction," says fifty-five-year-old Hal, who left his twenty-year marriage three years ago and is just finalizing the divorce. Hal has been seeing forty-one-year-old Cleo for the past two years. He loves their relationship, but isn't sure about marriage.

"I don't think Cleo can completely identify with what I'm going through. She's never been married. The thought of getting back into that is not a comfortable feeling for me. Cleo definitely has the right approach. She says, this marriage will be different. But what I find myself thinking is, all marriages are great at the beginning. Cleo has more of a time agenda than I do. She's never been married and she's worried about her age. Her expectations are reasonable, but I don't share her agenda. I'm still waiting for closure in the divorce. I need that. I've done all the hard work, I've worked through my fear of destroying my kids. But I honestly don't know where I'm headed."

Will you turn this keeper into a loser? Not if you take steps to prevent your own marriage fever from ruining the solid, loving, committed relationship you've already created. Cleo and Hal are approaching a turning point in their relationship. Although Cleo felt initially stung that after close to two years of involvement, Hal is reluctant to discuss marriage, she was unwilling to stay stung, to allow a temporary feeling of disappointment erode the loving connection she has with Hal.

"Emotionally, I've taken one step back," she says. "I love Hal, but I think he needs to experience his actual divorce. That's not unreasonable. He should experience that closure without feeling that I'm breathing down his neck. Now that Hal is about to become an available man, it's time for me to take a look at the relationship, too. If I'm being honest with myself, I have to acknowledge my own ambivalence. Hal's debt, for example. Suddenly, I'm thinking: Do I *want* to marry a man who's in debt and will continue to have substantial financial obligations to an ex-wife and two children? That's something for me to think about. Frankly, it's giving me pause. So just as he's saying to me, 'Look, I love you, but I need time to take a look around and see where I am,' I'm saying to him with just as much love and affection, 'I'm doing the same thing.' Now that it's almost possible, I have to decide if this is really how I see my life. Marriage is what I want. Now I have to figure out whether marriage to Hal is what I want. Our relationship is solid. But when the divorce actually happens, the future will be a brand-new blank page for both of us."

He makes an effort to normalize your relationship. How you could respond: *Normal? It isn't normal to have a relationship in which we don't socialize with his friends and he hasn't given me and his kids a chance to get to know each other. How can our relationship evolve if we can't be a normal couple?*

How you should respond: As long as he is not yet divorced, you can't be a normal couple—that is, a couple headed toward commitment in the conventional ways. That said, is he treating you like a much loved and valued girlfriend? Is he willing to commit to taking the relationship seriously? Do you have dates, spend weekends together, go to the movies and out to dinner? Maybe he's met all of your friends but you haven't met his. Ask him why. Who are the people he's close to? There's no reason to think he'd be in a big hurry to introduce you to couples who were a part of his marriage or even to his own family members, depending on the circumstances surrounding his divorce. As long as he's courting you and not treating your relationship as a secret affair for no reason, as long as he's not compartmentalizing you in some special little limited corner, you have as normal a relationship as you can have right now.

Will you turn this keeper into a loser? This is another place where you must try to let go of the way it's "supposed" to be. Remember: You're still on Divorce Time. Manage your anxiety. Do you have complaints? Try them out on a sensible girlfriend before you take them to him. Is he making the effort, given the special circumstances, of behaving like a good boyfriend? If he really is doing the best he can, under the circumstances, your glass is half-full. Don't tip it over.

He's shown you he can change. How you could respond: *You call this change? We talk about the need for him to negotiate harder (compromise more) with his wife (introduce me to his children/put a timeline on the divorce/speak to a therapist), but nothing has been definitively resolved.*

How you should respond: Remember, change is progress, not perfection. Recognizing the need for change *is* a step toward actually changing. Has he put the key into the ignition and started the motor? Maybe you need to move back into your own life a little more and give him a chance to catch up.

Will you turn this keeper into a loser? Sometimes the way to change a man is to perceive him differently. When Dorie and Sam, both forty-two, met walking their dogs in a neighborhood park, Sam had been separated eight months. His divorce, though amicable, was definitely in the slow lane, due to a novice mediator and a gridlocked court. That was okay with Sam who, up until the afternoon he met Dorie and her yellow Lab Fanny, had pretty much reconciled to a future consisting of a friendly enough ex-wife and Zip, his Jack Russell terrior. "Sam is a sweetheart, but he's allergic to change by temperament and always takes the path of least resistance," says Dorie. Dorie had never been married, but she knew something about men. "They want to be heroes." As Dorie and Sam fell in love—and Sam's divorce continued to limp along—Dorie made a point of letting Sam know she perceived him as doing everything in the best possible faith where she was concerned. "I was filling him with my optimism in us as a couple. I was saying, 'I know you're thinking about this and that I'm in good hands and that we're both going to come through this great.' I was telepathically pumping faith into him! It gave him the feeling that, where I was concerned, he could do no wrong. And therefore, he didn't." Close to three years after that chance meeting in the park, this couple married with both dogs as attendants.

He treats you as a valuable resource. How you could respond: *He tells me everything. Every day there's another chapter of his* *divorce drama to analyze. I'd like to go out to dinner and just laugh once in a while. I want to be his lover, not his therapist.*

How you should respond: His divorce *is* the central drama in his life. When he shares it with you, looks to you for support and listens to your take on things, he's telling you he values you. It's up to you to determine his level of commitment and whether his dependence on you is as tied to his future as it is to his day-to-day survival. Like it or not, you *are* a therapist, in a way. So be a good one. Consider your own time valuable. If he keeps telling you the same story without demonstrating a willingness to move forward, it's up to you to let him know he's wasting your time.

Will you turn this keeper into a loser? Don't make the mistake of valuing your relationship with him more than your relationship with yourself. If his divorce is getting you down, reclaim your life! If you don't like the way you sound when you're with him—whether it's your impatience with him or your enmeshment—take that step back. Tell him you need a small break, then take it. Guard against becoming embroiled in a competition with his wife. If you get too enmeshed—for example, by taking every opportunity to agree or convince him that she is a demon, you'll eventually pay for it. When he reconnects with his feelings of failure and loss, he could well blame you for the fallout of the divorce. It's a balancing act for you. Again, if you find yourself slipping, step away.

He respects your timeline. How you could respond: *Hey. The only way he can show me that he truly respects my timeline is by finalizing that divorce.*

How you should respond: *Okay, he doesn't totally control the big picture, but he is responsive to the small one. When we hit a snag, he makes the effort to devise a specific plan to help us move beyond it.*

Will you turn this keeper into a loser? When you're dating a divorcing man, there's a real temptation to frame each setback and frustration into an ultimatum: "If you won't please me by doing x, y, or z, I'm leaving you." There is a right time and a right way to deliver an ultimatum, but don't do it unless you're prepared to back it up. An ultimatum only has real impact once. Make sure you use it when you need it most. There's a difference between delivering an ultimatum and expressing a dissatisfaction. When something is happening in your relationship that you don't like— you never get to see him on weekends because he's with his kids or he hasn't really addressed the sticking points in the divorce negotiation—it's up to you to say, "This isn't a problem now, but if we don't deal with it it's going to become a problem." Only you know how much time overall you're able to invest in him before you run out of goodwill, patience, and self-respect. But don't overlook his efforts to deal with your day-to-day frustrations. They're an expression of his good faith.

Anya, who dated Gregg for three rocky years before his divorce became final, says it was Gregg's suggestion that they take a break for two months during that last year that ultimately preserved their relationship. "I was pretty strung out with the waiting," she says. "I loved Gregg, but it had gotten to where I was angry all the time. He said, 'Let's just stop for a while before we kill this.' I was uncertain of him at first, worried that he was backing out, but it turned out to be the best thing for us. He couldn't make the divorce happen any sooner, so he did what he could." Accept short-term solutions when you know they're offered in good faith. Give him credit for taking care of the relationship—he's doing what he can for now.

When you ask a question, he answers it. How you could respond: *But I don't like the answer he gives me.*

How you should respond: *What matters is that I can count on him giving me reliable information. If I don't like what I hear, I can act in my own best interests. I can make a decision based on good information.*

Will you turn a keeper into a loser? One of the biggest mistakes a woman can make in any romantic relationship—but especially in a relationship as complicated as that with a divorcing man—is to not ask questions. Why don't we ask? Sometimes it's because we want to avoid the consequences of unwelcome answers. Or we've confused asking a question with seeming demanding. As a result, being in love and exercising our right to good information seem mutually exclusive. Not so! A woman who asks straightforward questions—and the follow-up questions that go with those questions—may not always likes what she hears but she finds out fast if she's involved with a man willing to be straightforward with her. Just as important, she has a reality check, ammunition with which to counter the ups and downs of her own emotional states.

Ask and listen. Kelly, thirty-four, went so far as to write down what her boyfriend Richard told her. "I didn't trust myself during the early months of our romance," she says. "My family was horrified that I was dating a guy who was still married, and every time I tried to reassure them I found I didn't know what I needed to know. My sister, who I'm very close to, suggested that I write down questions—When was the divorce filed? When did he anticipate signing the final papers? What were the issues he was most concerned with pertaining to the divorce?—and his answers. I didn't tell Richard I was doing it, but it helped clarify my own perception of what was going on. He always told me as much as he knew. And if he didn't know, he told me that. It helped me to look at that piece of paper, stripped of all the emotions I was feeling, and to know that in January he said they were stuck negotiating monthly maintenance. So in April, when something else was happening, I could remember the history of that last negotiation. It sounds nitpicky, but it was a good exercise for me. It was just information. It couldn't hurt me. If Richard had refused to give me that information, that would have hurt me." If you don't have information, you can't construct a timeline for yourself. And if you can't construct a timeline, you can't give him information he needs about where *you* stand.

He's willing to negotiate a strategy for the immediate future.
What you could think: *But is he going to marry me after his divorce is final?*

How you should respond: A man who shows you that he is willing to commit to a plan—right now, today—that takes into account your thoughts, your ideas, and your timeline is the kind of man you *want* to spend a future with. In other words, narrow your focus to how he's treating you *now*. Naturally, if a man indicates to you that he's not up to a committed relationship with you in other ways (refer to this chapter's information about losers), factor it in. The point is, *you're* collecting information about him. And if he is present in the here-and-now of negotiating the immediate problems in your romance, trying to work out happy solutions for both of you, proceeding as if the two of you are a team, you've probably got a keeper.

Will you turn this keeper into a loser? What if one of your family members were seriously ill or in trouble and all your boyfriend could talk about was whether or not you think you'll have recovered sufficiently from the trauma six months from now to take a trip to France? Would you begin to get the feeling that your boyfriend didn't have too much empathy for what you were going through? On the other hand, how would you feel if he said something like, "Look, I know you're under a lot of stress, but how would you feel about spending a day in the country this weekend? I'd love to spend some time with you, and it might make you forget your troubles for a little while." Get your mind off your ultimate future with this man and start paying attention to today, tomorrow, and next week. Because today and tomorrow and next week *are* your relationship.

And don't forget your three choices:

- You can bail out of the relationship.

- You can put the relationship on hold.

- You can continue with the relationship.

DR. LESLIE PAM'S CHAPTER CHECKPOINTS

1. Share your own romantic history with him—your insights and your losses. See if he understands your stories. Have you been in a series of relationships while he's been married? Tell him your war stories. Show your own marriage scars. Educate him.

2. Does his behavior reflect who he says he is? He tells you he's a kind and wonderful man. Is he? Is that how you observe him?

3. Does he know who he is as well as what he is? Does he describe himself, for example, as "a lawyer who travels, likes snowboarding, rides a motorcycle"? As opposed to a man who is "happy, friendly, intense, demanding, sexy, and faithful"? Most men answer the what more easily than the who. Let him know why you think the who is equally important.

4. Is he looking for a new version of his wife? Even if he says he can't stand his old life, there are probably some qualities she has that he's still looking for. Unless he says they had nothing in common, you will probably be something like her, in terms of interests and enthusiasms. If they loved Third World traveling and you won't stay in anything less than a 5-star hotel, what will you do when he's no longer on his best behavior with you?

5. Is he still in love with the ideal of who his wife was? Is he in love with that memory? He has to let that idealized memory die. Give him space to mourn the death of that relationship, but make sure he has it in him to celebrate his new life with you.

6. Time off can mean a new chance. Take a few days or a few weeks away from the relationship if you think you're getting too enmeshed and needy. Return to your own life. Get a new perspective.

CHAPTER SIX

"You're Going to Love My Kids"

W HEN THIRTY-THREE-YEAR-OLD Chloe, a production assistant
in the film industry, met forty-one-year-old Tony at a barbe-
cue given by mutual friends, their first conversation was about his
kids and the impact his divorce—still ongoing—was having on
them. Tony's warmth and intensity attracted Chloe; so did that
fatherly concern. He'd been separated for barely a month, he told
her that afternoon. When he called her the next day to ask for a
date, he reassured Chloe that his marriage was definitely over, that
divorce papers had been filed. Chloe let him know that she was
skeptical—after all, he was still married and she had no interest in
dating a married man—but accepted his invitation for dinner and
a movie. That night, he brought along photos of his two children,
a sassy-looking girl of twelve and her fourteen-year-old sister with
freckles and an engaging grin. On their third date, Chloe detected
tears in Tony's eyes as he confessed over a romantic seaside lunch
how guilty he felt about putting his girls through the divorce, how
confusing the separation was for them. After lunch, as they walked
on the beach, Tony's cell phone rang three times.

First, his fourteen-year-old daughter just wanted to say she loved him. Then his twelve-year-old daughter called, checking to make sure he had stocked the videos she'd requested for the weekend. Then his older daughter called again, complaining that her mother wouldn't give her permission to invite a friend for a sleepover, insisting (Chloe could hear her emphatic tone of voice over the call of the seagulls) that her father intervene at once.

Tony smiled apologetically. "It's a way for me to feel connected," he told Chloe, slipping the phone into his pocket and taking her hand. Chloe felt as though she'd swallowed the sun whole. A mere month ago she'd have felt ill at the sight of a man taking a phone call on a beach. Now all she could think was: *What a loving, doting father. And, maybe someday* we'll *have a child together.* Tony's hand around hers felt so right, so strong and protective. It was a Daddy hand.

"Your girls sound darling," she told him. "So confident and assertive. I just know they'll come through this fine. I can't wait to meet them."

Tony gave her hand a reassuring squeeze. "You will," he promised. "Just as soon as the time is right."

WHEN SHOULD YOU MEET HIS KIDS?

As far as Chloe was concerned, she was ready to meet his girls that very weekend, in the first flush of their relationship. Chloe has two nieces she's crazy about and she loves kids. Furthermore, kids are drawn to Chloe's sweet playfulness and easy warmth. More to the point, Chloe was already wildly smitten with Tony—and, therefore, ready and willing to feel smitten with his kids. Also, Chloe knew that by introducing her to his kids, Tony would be making a statement about his feelings for her. As the weeks went by, Chloe became more and more eager to hear that statement. Meeting Tony's kids—having them welcome her into their lives—had begun to feel as crucial to her future as Tony's divorce.

Chloe loves kids, but maybe you don't. Or maybe you've met his kids, adore them, and they just aren't warming up to you. Or you might be wondering why he's postponing this important meeting. Perhaps you have children of your own who are or will become an element in this relationship. Wherever you are in the divorcing-man-and-his-kids story, you know that finessing this plot point is crucial to your new relationship. Even if his children are adults with children of their own, there are repercussions whenever a parent brings a new romantic partner into children's lives. These are some of the variables you'll be taking into account:

- How old are his kids?

- How recent is his separation?

- How familiar are his kids with their father's dating behavior?

- Does he customarily introduce his kids to casual girlfriends?

- Has he told his children that he's seeing someone special?

- Have his children expressed a desire to meet you?

Go Slow and Keep Your Eyes Open

Psychologists and divorce lawyers agree that when it comes to introducing children to an important new woman in their dad's life, it's always best—best for the kids and therefore best for your relationship—if you move slowly. Especially in situations where the kids are school age, both his separation from their mother and his relationship with you should be well-established. Some experts suggest waiting six months minimum after a separation for that first introduction. But every situation will have its unique circumstances. If he's been out of the house seven months and has only been seeing you for a week, meeting the kids is probably premature. The "right time" to meet his kids refers just as crucially to the point at which you and he have established a committed relationship. This means that you're dating exclusively, hopeful about a shared future, and trying to work out your problems together; it doesn't necessarily mean you've made plans to marry or even that the subject's come up. Attorneys and psychologists agree that a man can easily hide dates and casual sex from his kids, but once a woman becomes an ongoing and important part of his life, it's a mistake to hide that relationship from his kids. That said, it's up to the two of you to decide how you want to characterize your relationship to the children. Tanya, thirty-eight, met Joe's two young children on a summer weekend at his beach house and was introduced as a friend. "The children were staying with him for the weekend, and Joe invited me as well as two other friends," she says. "I was part of the group. I slept in a separate bedroom. Little by little, they accepted me as one of their daddy's friends, then when I was a little more familiar to them, we spent time with them as a couple. Still, we stayed in separate bedrooms until the divorce was final. That just felt more comfortable to me."

When in doubt, err on the side of caution—meaning, put the interests of the children first. However much you love him and however eager you are to love his children, keep in mind two overriding realities if they're underage:

1. Their best interests come first, not yours.

2. Chances are good their first response to you will be negative.

These realities may be hard to swallow. After all, you have no emotional attachment to or investment in these children. But you do have an emotional investment in him. Your goal is to help him help his kids cope with your new place in his life. Ultimately, whatever serves his relationship with his kids and the resolution of the divorce *is* good for you and good for your relationship. Here, as always, our advice remains the same: *Don't play it safe, play it sane.* You don't have to wait passively. You can actively influence this passage, and you should. You can have a big say in making sure this meeting happens in a timely and proper manner—for you, for him, and for the kids.

When You're the One Who Wants to Wait

Maybe you don't want to be involved with his children until there's some public announcement of your relationship, like an engagement. There's nothing wrong with that. Charlotte, twenty-seven, an illustrator, fell in love with Rod, a forty-one-year-old architect with three children under ten, less than six months into his separation. Rod adored his kids, and as he and Charlotte became close, he wanted her to meet them. Charlotte was reluctant, not entirely certain why herself. "When I thought about it more, I realized that I didn't want to meet his kids—to become a part of their lives and vice versa—until and unless Rod and I were engaged, or otherwise publicly official about our intentions toward each other," she says. "There seemed to be too much at stake." Charlotte told Rod that she'd like to postpone a meeting until they knew each other better. After more time went by, she let him know the full extent of her feelings about waiting. Rod respected those feelings. His divorce became final within another seven months, and he and Charlotte announced their engagement shortly thereafter, at which time she finally met his children.

It's equally wise to slow him down if he wants you and the kids to become acquainted too quickly. Marisa, a thirty-four-year-old, never-married financial analyst with sleek Gwyneth Paltrow looks, met thirty-two-year-old Barry, a fundraiser for a museum, a few months after his separation. After Marisa and Barry had dated three times, Barry invited her to meet his kids during the upcoming weekend. "I was flattered, but wary," says Marisa. "Barry and I were having a terrific time—over three wonderful dinners and an afternoon together, we'd definitely become excited about spending time together. But meeting his two small children? I felt it was too soon. I didn't want to hurt Barry's feelings, but I felt we should wait and I told him my feelings."

Marisa's instincts were good. If you've only just met a man, don't assume that an immediate invitation to get involved with his kids means he has your interests or his kids' interests at heart. Maybe the guy is at a loss about how to occupy his children dur- ing weekend visits, and it relieves his anxiety to have a woman step in and help out. Although it's flattering, it's too soon. You haven't established the boundaries of your own relationship. Watch his response when you slow him down. Barry's reaction didn't sit well with Marisa. "I could see that he was a little angry," she says. "He wanted me there." That reaction suggested to her that Barry was thinking less about his kids than about his own needs. "We dated for a little longer, but I ultimately found him immature and some- what selfish."

Is He Overly Protective?

Chloe, who dutifully removed her extra makeup and clothing from Tony's bathroom and bedroom for every impromptu sleep- over and scheduled weekend visit, was becoming impatient as the months went by. Tony spent so much time with the children, yet he wasn't ready for her to meet them. What was Tony waiting for? She respected Tony for being protective of his kids' feelings— Tony and Chloe were still finding their way as a twosome and hadn't exactly talked about a future together. Also, Tony's divorce was far from final. It would be irresponsible of Tony to bring his girls into a romantic relationship that wasn't rock-solid. They'd already warned him how they'd react. "We'll just make her life miserable, Dad," his younger daughter had said with straightforward simplicity.

But isn't it possible to be *too* cautious?

Yes. Tony felt so guilty about the failure of his marriage that he was having difficulty finding a healthy way to separate enough from his children in order to develop a relationship with Chloe. As it turned out, Chloe didn't meet Tony's kids for another five months.

QUESTIONS TO ASK HIM ABOUT HIS CHILDREN

How are you to determine whether he's moving you into his children's lives too fast or too slow, if he's making a statement about his intentions toward you, or is so anxious himself about single-parenting that he'll bring any new woman into his kids' lives? It's up to you to figure that out. When you begin dating a man with children, be sure to ask questions. Some of these are the same questions you'd ask any new man.

- Do you have children?

- How many?

- How old are they?

- How often do you see them?

Sit back and wait for his responses. "I have two wonderful children and I'm really close to them," he says. Your follow-up questions can then be more pointed:

● What makes you feel close to them?

● What kinds of things do you do with them?

Really pay attention to his answers. You can tell by the way a man talks about his kids how involved he actually is in their school lives, their extra-curricular activities, their friendships. If, like Tony, he's feeling guilty and having trouble separating, you'll sense it in his over-concern.

On the other hand, if he's barely involved at all, you also want to know why. It's part of reading a man emotionally—and weighing whether he'll be a good father if the two of you decide to have children of your own.

If You're Feeling Jealous of His Children

It's okay if you are. After all, his kids were there before you, they devour his time and his attention and, financially, they're a burden. But: You *must* know yourself well enough to be able to recognize these feelings. You have to admit to yourself whether jealous feelings are coloring your perceptions of his relationship with them. Does he seem overly protective and involved because he is, or do you see him that way because you don't want to share him? Sometimes it's a little of both.

Vicky, thirty-six, had been dating Mark, fifty-five, for eight months when she met his eight-year-old daughter and twelve-year-old son. "I felt that Mark spoiled his kids out of guilt—as a result, they were little monsters, demanding everything, completely undisciplined," says Vicky. "They rode roughshod over him. When we went out with the kids, they demanded the front seat of the car, hung on their father, and he indulged every temper tantrum. I felt as if I had to let them know that they couldn't be in charge of our relationship. I was always holding Mark's hand, trying to make a statement, like: 'Listen up, kids. *I'm* the new kid in town.' My instinct was to claim my territory. I handled it all wrong. The kids didn't need any added incentive to resent me, and Mark got caught in the middle. Ultimately we fell apart over these kids. You can't compete with the divorce, and you shouldn't even try to compete with his children."

You also can't interfere in the money he spends on his kids. Even if it's hard to watch, you have to keep your mouth shut. You can ask, "Hey, do you think it's appropriate to buy him a new car when he's totaled two?" That's a parental issue, not a money issue. You can't say, "You spend money on him and we haven't gone on vacation." You're the girlfriend. He doesn't owe it to you, but he does owe it to his kids. Again, you have to look at everything from the kids' point of view—not yours, not his, not his wife's. You have to put their interests first.

Keep in mind that a man who is absent from his kids a lot because he's with his girlfriend isn't going to make a great impression on a judge who's deciding visitation and custody issues. If he's always canceling visitation because he wants to take you skiing, that could be a problem. It's in your own long-range best interests to recognize and manage whatever jealousy or possessiveness you might be feeling. You don't want him to blame you later for ruining his relationship with his children.

YOU ARE NOW ENTERING THE HOT ZONE

Up until you meet the children, it's possible that your boyfriend's wife has known little about his dating life. When the kids meet you, the news blackout is officially over. If the mother is the one who wanted the divorce or if she has someone in her life, chances are it's not going to be a problem. There are millions of women out there who want every other weekend free. They want to do their own thing—go scuba diving, throw pots in Mexico.

Suddenly they have a free babysitter. Don't assume it's going to be a fight. Sometimes this information brings only relief.

But sometimes it's like throwing gasoline on a fire.

JULIA'S STORY

I met Arthur's two kids, a five-year-old boy and a fourteen-year-old girl, eight months after we became involved. All along, Arthur never stopped talking about how much the kids were going to love me. He said they were just like me—young and fun and adorable. Arthur and his wife were out-of-control where these kids were concerned. The children were little tyrants, no doubt because of their parents. His wife was constantly switching plans on Arthur, jerking both him and the kids around because she was so angry. Arthur's daughter was shockingly rude to her father, who never corrected her. Their mother knew about me and filled the kids' heads with how awful I was. There was a lot of money involved in this divorce, and Arthur had been the one who wanted out of the marriage.

Finally, his daughter said she was dying to meet me, so we set up a restaurant meeting. I had already semi-moved in with Arthur, but his therapist suggested that I move out now that I was meeting the kids. I did. We arranged to meet at a small restaurant. I was there with a girlfriend. Arthur stopped by our table with the kids, and we all pretended it was a chance encounter. His daughter was lovely, a little reserved toward me, and extremely possessive of her father. His little boy was sweet. We continued to go slow, letting them know I was Arthur's friend, setting up a few more casual meetings, spending a little more time together with them.

The x-factor was Arthur's wife, who continued to behave erratically, causing the kids to act out and behave like monsters. Once when Arthur and I were on vacation, she put the kids on a plane and, totally without warning, sent them to stay with us.

A couple months later, I moved back in with Arthur. That's when things escalated out of control. The kids called all the time to report another crisis with their mother—she took too many pills or she was afraid she had cancer or she had locked them in their room and wouldn't let them out. The worse she behaved, the worse the kids behaved.

Eventually it wore me down. It wasn't the kids' fault—they were caught in the middle of this divorce with neither parent really looking out for their interests. But it turned me into a shrew. I was as angry and bitter and intolerant as his wife. I couldn't stand myself.

My only relief was the little trips Arthur and I took. They were an oasis for both of us. Arthur and I seemed to be fighting all the time now. I couldn't stand the way his kids walked all over him. We had a four-day trip scheduled—it was to celebrate my birthday—and the day before we were supposed to leave, Arthur told me the trip was off because of a change of plans involving the kids. I just lost it. Once you get to that place where everything makes you angry—even if you have a right to be— it doesn't matter. I just couldn't do it any longer. I realized that his divorce was going to drag on for another couple years. I was too worn down. I moved out. Eventually, I moved to the other side of the country. The last I heard, one of the kids is in drug rehab and Arthur has moved back in with his wife.

Find Your Own—and Their—Comfort Zone

Here's the reality. In the early stages of a divorce, children are like- ly to be needy, hostile, and acting out to beat the band. That said, it's not your responsibility to make his kids love you. Don't court them effusively. If friendly and warm is your style, be so, but let them ask you the questions. If you like children, let them know that you do. Give them a chance to see how they feel. (Sometimes kids are feeling so starved for their father's attention that they'll love you just for being with them.) Even if you've waited months for the meeting, expect the kids to be somewhat uncomfortable and uptight. Children are all ego. Their paramount concern is: How will this person affect *me*? What they need to know is that their dad will still be there for them, despite your presence in his life. When Candace, a savvy and secure twelve-year-old, met her father's girlfriend, Lily, she was immediately drawn to her. "I think she'll make a great stepmom," she told her father, then added, "But if you marry her, will we see you as much as we do now? Or will we see less of you?"

Assume that children have these fears, even if they don't express them. Most kids don't deal easily with meeting the girlfriend, even if they don't show it. They have mixed feelings of loyalty; they feel as though they're in a bind. Younger children often get recruited as spies by the other parent. Teenaged girls who may be at odds with their own mother right now might see you, the girlfriend, as a way to help them express some of that hostility. Children can be manipulative.

If his wife has a boyfriend the kids have met, that's a good precedent. "My boyfriend's wife was the first one to get involved after their separation," says thirty-eight-year-old Elaine. "His daughter hated the guy—he tried too hard to win her over. I was the beneficiary of all his mistakes. I realized I had to be very low-key with her, to let her set the pace, and that's what I did." Again, it depends on how the kids are doing and their ages. You can explain more to a thirteen-year-old than a four-year-old. Take them out to dinner, take them to the zoo. Don't invite them to spend the weekend with you for the first visit. When he has visitation early in the separation, he has to spend time with them. Taking them out to lunch on Saturday afternoon to a fancy restaurant because you love it isn't going to win their affection.

Callie, thirty-six, connected quickly to her boyfriend Danny's two daughters, one thirteen and the other sixteen, because she was sensitive to the subtleties from the beginning. "Even when the four of us walked down the street, for example, I made a point of letting the girls have pride of place next to their father. I hung back a little, taking my cue from them. I think that let them know that I wasn't a threat to them. I didn't want them to feel displaced for one second." On the other hand, it's a mistake for him or you to give too much control and responsibility to the children. You're still the adults. You don't have to ride in the backseat of the car.

HIS CHALLENGE: TO MOVE PAST GUILT AND REDEFINE HIS ROLE AS A DAD

The man you love is likely to be a pitiful wreck of a human specimen when it comes to his feelings about his children. Whatever complicated mess of conflicting emotions he's hauling around about his wife and his marriage, when it comes to his children, this man is a simple and straightforward creature.

He's guilty, guilty, guilty.

This guilt is almost as painful to watch as it is to experience. You can see it eating away at his self-esteem, corroding his confidence. You can feel his anguish. The tape that runs inside and outside his head has become a kind of mantra. *Oh, my God,* he tells you and himself. *I am never going to be a decent father. My children will hate me forever. They will never understand. Oh, my God.*

Your heart breaks for this man. And, needless to say, ministering to this guilt is not the way you imagined spending your Saturday nights.

But before you get to the bottom of that box of Kleenex, let us point out that there's another tape running in your man's head. This tape is connected to a calculator. It goes something like this: *I'm a moral failure but, even worse, I'm a financial catastrophe. Why didn't my wife and I have a prenup? My kids need twice as much as they ever did before. Not only a second home, but enough expensive sneakers and electronic equipment to fill it. She* (you) *wants us to travel! She expects nice dinners out every single week-end! Not only do I have less disposable income than ever, but I have to share it with her! If we get married, I'll need even more money! And she wants us to start a second family? Oh, my God, what if we get divorced?*

Maybe your back goes up at the sound of such cold logic. He's in love with you: You're the Red Cross and Cindy Crawford all rolled up into one delicious gift-wrapped package. How could he be thinking such calculating thoughts? Frankly, you'd rather hear the guilty tape.

No, you wouldn't. His guilt over his kids and his marriage isn't just painful—it's the enemy of your relationship.

Your Challenge: To Help Him See Opportunity Where He Sees Failure

What Chloe couldn't know those early weeks of her relationship with Tony was the history of his relationship with his two kids. When Tony's fifteen-year marriage began, he was struggling to get a small retail business on its feet in southern California. Like a lot of men, Tony poured the bulk of his time and energy into his work. Supporting his family was vital to his self-worth as a man—especially one of Italian descent. He worked hard for his kids, just the way his own father had. Family was everything, he'd readily tell anyone who asked. But his marriage, to a woman he'd been dating since high school, was eroding. By the time his daughter was born, the disconnections in Tony's marriage had gone unacknowledged for too long. Tony loved his little girl, and when his second daughter was born two years later, he was ecstatic and proud. By then, Tony's business had become successful, and he was working twice as hard to keep it that way. So he missed the ballet recitals and the birthday parties and the goodnight stories. (Hadn't his own father raised six kids without ever attending a single school play?) When his daughters were ten and eight, Tony had an affair with one of his suppliers. It didn't last long, but it cracked his view of his marriage—emotionally arid and sexually stale—wide open. He struggled silently for another year, then told his wife he wanted to move out. He wanted a divorce. She was distraught and frantic. His older daughter was hysterical. His younger daughter began wetting her bed. Tony and his wife tried therapy, then a trial reconciliation, then more therapy. Finally, Tony moved out for good, one daughter clutching at his shirttails and begging to be taken with him, the other sobbing in her room. Four months later, he met Chloe.

A man who spends his relationship with you lamenting the terrible trauma he's inflicted upon his children, a man who sees his guilt as a barrier between him and all forward movement, is not a man about to fall onto his knees and beg for your hand in marriage. You might see that final divorce document as all that stands between you and your future, but you're as wrong as can be. That document is nothing compared to his feelings of guilt and failure where his kids are concerned. Unless he can move beyond that guilt, your relationship is doomed. A man who is stuck on guilt is stuck in the past, and that's not a place where a loving, healthy relationship with you—or with his kids—is ever going to take root and bloom.

Chloe didn't understand why Tony had to compartmentalize her so completely. His wife knew he was "dating." Why shouldn't Chloe meet the kids? Tony countered by saying he didn't want his wife knowing how serious he and Chloe were becoming. If the kids knew all about Chloe, so would his wife. Tony wasn't being disingenuous—he meant what he said—but his motives were more complicated. Leaving his marriage had created so much emotional chaos that to up the guilt ante by having both his kids and his wife resent the growing importance of another woman in his life was an event he automatically shrank from. He was falling in love with Chloe and fantasizing about a future with her, but the guilt was more persuasive than the fantasy. His gut told him to put off the meeting.

Chloe's Choices

How could Chloe help Tony deal with his guilt and, by doing so, move their relationship forward? How can you help the man you love work through the tangle of parental emotions that threatens your future together?

- Not by manipulating him. ("You're just using me, you don't really care. If you really cared as much as you say you do, you'd want me to meet your children.") Manipulation might work short-term, but it will never get you where you really want to be.

- Not by demanding that he get over it. ("I've been with you for six months and haven't met your kids yet. This is ridiculous. You have to take control of your life.") More pressure is the last thing he needs.

You help move him beyond guilt by helping him feel hopeful—about his future with you and about the opportunity he now has to create an entirely new—even better—relationship with his kids.

You help him by trying to effect a change in his attitude.

You help him by acknowledging change—however small—when it occurs.

TRUTH TIME: HOW STUCK IS HE?

Imagine that the two of you plan to drive to the country for the weekend. You get into the car. He's in the driver's seat. You wait for him to put the key into the ignition. He just sits there.

"So?" you say. "What are you waiting for?"

"I'm afraid it might rain," he says.

"That's okay," you say. "We'll turn on the windshield wipers."

Still, he sits there.

"I thought you wanted to go the country," you say.

"I do," he says. "I really want to go to the country."

"So why aren't you starting the car?" you say.

"We might not have enough gas," he says.

"We'll stop and fill up the tank first," you say.

Nothing.

Your voice rises. "Put the key in the ignition!" you insist. "How do you expect us to go anywhere unless you start the car?"

Do you have an exclusive and ongoing relationship with him? If so, and he's committed to a relationship for now, he should be ready and willing to introduce you to his kids. He should be ready to move forward. Is he? Not if you keep hearing the following:

"The timing is wrong."

"My wife will go ballistic."

"The therapist says . . ."

"Let's just keep things the way they are for now."

"I'm not ready."

Can You Tell Him What You See?

You'll never get where you want to go unless he puts that key into the ignition. You can't be with a man who won't take that step. If he's stuck in one spot, he's stuck in the past. If your relationship is standing still, it's automatically falling behind. Meeting his kids is one way to define forward progress. If you meet his kids, does that mean he'll get his divorce and the two of you will get married and live happily ever after? No. It means that he's willing to make a change. It means that he's making forward progress. It means that if he was 100 percent stuck, now he's 98 percent stuck.

Change is progress, not perfection.

So what do you do when he won't put the key into the ignition? You apply the following principle: *Can I say what I see about you?*

Chloe was fed up. She'd been seeing Tony exclusively for five months. She'd heard him lament his sorry relationship with his children in a thousand different ways. She'd watched from the sidelines as his wife made or canceled last-minute plans for the kids to spend time with him. Chloe and Tony had already established the kind of relationship in which Chloe felt free to speak her mind. Now she did just that. Here is what she told Tony:

"We've been together for five months. We have an intimate, loving, sexual relationship. When you keep me separate from your kids, you exclude me from your life. If you can't tell me what I can do to help us move forward or what conditions would have to prevail for me to be a part of your family, you're telling me that I can't be in a relationship with you. I understand the financial aspects of this step. I understand that your wife might not be completely thrilled with the idea of me in the kids' lives. I'm not asking to mother your kids. But if you're committed to our relationship for now, I have to be a part of your ongoing life—and your ongoing life includes your kids."

A man who responds to such sentiments by getting angry, by stonewalling, by walking away, or by continuing the mantra of don't-pressure-me-I'm-not-ready is a man who won't put that key into the ignition.

Tony didn't do that. He acknowledged Chloe's need for change. Here's what Tony said:

"You're right. I'm stuck. I don't know how to get unstuck, but I'd like to try. Maybe we can talk about planning a first meeting. Let's start there, then see how it goes."

Real progress happens when a man can listen to your point of view, recognize it as valid, and take it into consideration. That man is capable of change. That doesn't mean he's rushing out to give it a great big hug. This is hard. He's probably going to procrastinate.

Another month went by, and still Tony hadn't come up with a plan. This is what Chloe said then:

"A month ago we talked about getting to a place where I could meet your kids. I was wondering if you felt we were there yet. I've given the meeting some thought, and I'm ready to talk it through and do it. Is there something you still need to do?"

Real change occurs when a person's attitude shifts. To move from "I can't" or "I won't" to "I'll try to be different tomorrow" is a leap from hopelessness to hopefulness. When the two of you fight, you only want to feel hopeful, to feel that things can be different, that change is possible. If you can keep him in a hopeful state, if you can address these issues without making him feel hopeless, you can move forward. Do you believe that participating in this process, influencing it, helping it happen is a form of cheating? Do you believe that unless all forward movement is generated by him, it must mean he doesn't love you or want the relationship enough? If you do, you're sunk. Get over it. If the two of you have an exclusive, committed-for-now relationship, you can and should be using everything in your power to influence it.

Remember the mantra: *Don't play it safe, play it sane.*

Chloe suggested a few possible options for a meeting: An informal meeting on the beach, a costume exhibit at the museum, a gathering at Tony's home. Both daughters had already overheard telephone conversations between their dad and a friend named Chloe. They knew that the same friend had made a music tape for their father's car. When Tony mentioned that his business partner and family friend's birthday was coming up, Chloe spotted an opportunity. Why didn't Tony arrange a small party, inviting a few people the kids already knew, including the children of his partner, and Chloe. Tony balked. He thought it would be uncomfortable. But Chloe was sure it would work. It did. The girls gravitated to Chloe immediately.

The next day the older daughter demanded to know, "Is she your girlfriend, Dad?"

"Yeah, I guess you could say that," Tony said.

"Cool," she said.

Now remember, you're not there yet. And you still have the same three options:

- You can bail out of the relationship.

- You can put the relationship on hold.

- You can continue with the relationship.

DR. LESLIE PAM'S CHAPTER CHECKPOINTS

1. Keep an open mind about his kids. Don't let his descriptions of who they are and what they're like color your impressions.

2. Don't demand to meet his children. Wait for an opening. Then ask: "Does this seem like the right time to you?" If he hasn't seen them himself for a week or longer, let him spend time with them first. It takes time for "stranger" feelings to wear off, even between him and his kids. Let them spend the day or night with him first. Then enter the equation.

3. Have a debriefing with him after the first meeting. Your first question shouldn't be "What did they think of me?" Let him offer his impressions of how the meeting went. Remember that they have preconceived notions of you before they meet you. They've talked about you with their dad. You don't know what they've discussed and don't need to know—it's a family conversation.

4. If they don't like you—and even if they do like you—don't take it personally. No one will be 100 percent comfortable or real at that first meeting. It's an artificial relationship at first.

5. Expect the first meeting to be strained and stressful. If the atmosphere doesn't ease up on the second meeting, take a break and try again later.

6. Be wary of the man with too many instructions about what to say and do and how to behave with his kids. You will fail, and he will bail! This man will be using you to deal with his guilt. Look for him to acknowledge that your opinions and advice are valid.

7. Don't advise him about his parenting skills unless he asks. Do let him know what makes you comfortable or uncomfortable. For example, "When you let your son yell and scream and hit you, I felt really uncomfortable because you just sat there and let him do it." Or, "It was great to see how much affection you show with your kids. I can see you really love and care about them."

8. Establish your own independent relationship with his kids. After that first meeting, send a card or make a phone call. Present yourself as an individual separate from their dad.

CHAPTER SEVEN

How to Be Heart-Smart When Love Hurts

W HAT IS IT ABOUT love that sometimes makes us stupid? Can a person with a brain intact still be in love? Or do you suspect that "smart love" is "safe love" in disguise, a matter of giving up Lancelot the Hot for Harold the Dull? It's not cheating to fall in love with your brain turned *on*. Leave your brain behind when you fall in love with a divorcing man, and you might as well be bungee jumping without the cord.

Smart love is still love, thrills and all, but wiser, more focused, more observant. Let your heart be sweetly distracted by promise and possibility. Just keep a cool third eye in place to weigh the evidence, evaluate the facts, and draw a few conclusions. And what if the man you're with turns out to be the man you're better off without? Smart love will deliver you to the wonderful man in your future, faster and in better shape to appreciate him.

When you fall in love with a separated man, playing dumb doesn't cut it. It's not merely a matter of keeping that third eye peeled for all the usual love ambushes—it's that the ambushes themselves take more of a toll. Your love lows are lower than they are in the usual love affair. That's because each time you hit even a medium-sized love bump, your disappointment, anxiety, and frustration are compounded by the larger uncertainty—his ongoing divorce—and your pain is intensified.

Granted, no love affair goes smoothly. In fact, if you haven't experienced hurt and frustration in a romance, you haven't experienced intimacy either. That doesn't mean you don't have a choice. Play it smart, and you'll keep the *conflict du jour* from utterly derailing your self-esteem and your connection with him. In this chapter, we'll describe common love snags that have tripped up other women in your situation and tell you how to finesse them to your relationship's advantage.

Our point here is, as always: *Don't play it safe, play it sane.* You are not a victim of his divorce circumstances, so stop wringing your hands and bemoaning your fate! You're not only the lead actor in your own drama, you're writing the script as well. You chose a difficult situation, but you can continue to have smart choices along the way. It's in your power to transform these hot buttons from setbacks to opportunities—for deeper self-knowledge as well as a stronger bond with the man you love.

HE'S STILL CLOSE TO HIS WIFE

Caroline, forty-two, a pretty, curly-haired financial analyst, considered herself a wised-up romantic realist when she fell in love with forty-three-year-old Marvin, a soft-spoken pharmaceutical executive, eight months into his separation from his wife of twenty-two years. "I was never married, but I'd had several long-term relationships," says Caroline. "Marvin was the sweetest man I'd ever been involved with. I felt blessed. Even though he wasn't divorced, I knew I'd found a good man. His marriage ended with lots of pain on both sides, but it was definitely over. By the time we met, he'd been through so much. After a lot of anger, Marvin and his wife were try-

ing to behave rationally with each other in order to move the divorce along and be good parents to their teenaged son." One weekend, Caroline and Marvin went away. On Sunday morning, Marvin called his wife from the hotel to make arrangements for picking up his son when they got back. "I had just stepped out of the shower and I was toweling my hair when I heard the sound of Marvin's voice— that low, intimate voice he used only with me. I was stunned to realize that he was talking to his wife. His wife!" Stunned and jealous. "I felt hurt. How was it possible that he still had that same degree of intimacy with her? It didn't seem right to me. When he hung up, I told him how I felt. I suggested that maybe his divorce was still dragging on because he hadn't really separated emotionally from his wife." They argued, and the incident passed. But it left misunderstanding on both sides. "I felt insecure and fearful. Marvin was defensive. It changed the way I felt about us."

Myth: His bond with his wife is a threat to your relationship.

Reality: Jealousy is a tricky emotion to deal with in any love affair. When you're involved with a still-married man, jealousy is especially perilous and all too common. After all, his soon-to-be ex is always a presence. You've been lulled into thinking of her as a negative presence—the human embodiment of all that stands between your and his happiness—until you have an experience like the one Caroline describes. Then, suddenly you're face-to-face with a troubling and dissonant reality: He *was* intimate with this other woman. Maybe he still is. How will you deal with that? You're not the first woman he's been intimate with. Moreover, if he has children, he and his wife are going to be parents together— meaning, he's going to have a relationship with her—for the rest of their (and your) lives.

Insight: Your insecurity—greater or lesser, depending on how stalemated you feel right now in this relationship—is creating the jealousy.

Action: Don't confront him, confront yourself. Cry out your own feelings in private if you have to and get them out of the way.

Then include him in your confrontation with yourself. Tell him: "I'm surprised at how hurt I felt hearing your conversation with her. But I realize that I'm not the first person in your life, and you're not the first man in mine." This is a different conversation than the angry one you were tempted to have with him. This conversation has the potential to draw you closer rather than pull you apart. When you tell another person what *they're* feeling rather than what *you're* feeling, you miss an opportunity to be intimate.

Silver Lining: You've been given an opportunity to see your man's relationship history in action. You've been given a glimpse of how loving and intimate he's capable of being with a woman— even a woman he's in the process of divorcing! He knows how to be intimate. Count your blessings. Lots of men don't.

HE SAYS HE'LL DO SOMETHING, AND THEN HE DOESN'T FOLLOW THROUGH

Jessica, a forty-year-old mother of two and a commercial property realtor, met forty-nine-year-old Howard, a cosmetic company executive, just as her divorce was becoming final. Howard had been separated for close to a year, but his divorce negotiations were bogged down in financial complexities and acrimony. "I was sympathetic at first because I'd just been through a divorce myself," says Jessica. "As Howard and I became more deeply involved, though, I really had a hard time. Howard was all bravado—lots of pumped-up talk about how he intended to handle his wife, his lawyer, his time—but then, more often than not, he'd totally wimp out and just take the path of least resistance. The path of least resistance always seemed to lead to me getting shortended. If I say I'm going to do something, I do it. I tried my best to make him feel stronger, to make him stand up for us. Why couldn't he? We'd been seeing each other for several months, and though I trusted his feelings for me, I started thinking, maybe this guy really isn't worth it."

Myth: If he can't be one hundred percent consistent, you're wasting your time.

Reality: The man you love has feet of clay. He will disappoint you.

Insight: You're tempted to confront him: "You said you were going to tell your wife you couldn't see her tomorrow! I guess you don't have as much of a handle on your divorce as you say you do!" You're tempted to try and make him stronger: "You have the facts on your side! Just approach her with confidence, and don't let her out-talk you!" These approaches aren't effective, though. You need to give him a chance to fail, to let him know that he doesn't have to be perfect. Instead, tell him he doesn't have to prove anything to you. If he has to keep coming back to you to say he didn't make the grade too many times, he's going to start making things up just to look good. Aim for higher ground, for a deeper degree of honesty. Give him the opportunity to say, "I guess I don't have it as together as I'd like." Be straight with each other about the disappointment.

Action: So where does that leave you? With a choice, as always. How you handle your disappointment is entirely your call, your choice. Double messages can keep you in a relationship longer than you might find comfortable. Make a list: He said this. He did this. If his statements and his actions are always inconsistent, it doesn't really matter what his reasons are. He says he wants to be with you for the rest of his life because you make him so happy. Then he cancels his vacation plans with you because his children were expecting him to take them on a vacation alone. He'd rather spend an evening watching a video and eating takeout with you than anything else he can think of. Then his wife needs him to attend a cocktail party with her because it's a long-standing charity event obligation. "With Robert, his mantra was, "My kids come first,'" says Kylie, forty. "Okay, I understood what he meant—until it was the reason he was postponing making our holiday plans because he was concerned about how the kids would feel. That wasn't acceptable to me. I told him, either we're a couple or we're not. If we are, we can work out the issues with the kids together. But you can't push me to the bottom of the list because it's more comfortable, then put it off on the kids. If I'd left it to him, he'd have chosen the path of least resistance. I didn't, so he had to force himself to actually make holiday plans that included me and took into account their concerns."

It's not wrong of him to choose his children or a cocktail party with his wife over you, but from your point of view they are not good reasons why he can't be with you. It's the inconsistency you're up against, not the facts. Take action against the inconsistency, not the man. Here's the kind of statement you need to hear from him: "There will be times when I choose my children over you. That's how it is right now." Now it's up to you. You can choose to say okay. You can choose to say, that doesn't work for me. Maybe he'll never be able to choose you over his kids or his wife. How will you feel about that? Again, you can choose to say okay. Calculate the cost to you, based on your own tolerance. Don't blame him. Assigning blame makes you a victim.

Silver Lining: If you're not having conflict, you're not having an intimate relationship. Speak your mind and choose your course of action based on what he offers you at any given moment. If you continue to speak the truth of your feelings and allow him to do the same, then deal with the conflict and choices as they present themselves—rather than mute your true self in manipulation or silence—and you will come out on top *even if this relationship doesn't work out.*

HE'S NOT FAIR ABOUT HIS TIME

Josie, thirty, a social worker, had a brief marriage as a twenty-three-year-old graduate student. Divorced, she's been seeing Bradley, also a social worker in her community, for three months. Josie and Bradley met at a senior citizens center. Bradley had moved out of his house a month before Josie and he met. "We saw each other platonically for the first two months," says Josie. "I knew he'd just left his wife, and I couldn't see getting involved with him. It was too volatile a situation. He has a small daughter and his wife doesn't sound all that stable, which I can't blame her for, considering the fact that her husband just left her." But the connection between Josie and Bradley felt too special to ignore. The friendship blossomed, and they became lovers. "Now I'm in the very situation I feared. I feel deprived of time with him and that I'm being treated unfairly. Bradley says that he has to placate his wife, that he has to see his daughter—and I understand that he does have to do those things—but it still feels bad when I get the short end of the stick."

Myth: When you date a divorcing man, you're signing on for second-place. You have to expect to come second to his children and to all matters relating to the divorce.

Reality: Your time is valuable.

Insight: Again, it's not a question of whether it's "right" for him to put you behind his children or the necessities of the divorce. It's about fairness. It's not fair of him to continue to fit you in when he has time. He must recognize that your time is valuable to you. This is about a choice that the two of you can make together.

Action: Tell him: "I need a couple of days notice if you're going to change our plans. You can't call me at the last minute." If that doesn't work for him? Suggest that for the next two months (or however long you decide) you see him every other weekend, while he works this out. Ask him: "Will that work for you?" He can say yes or no.

Silver Lining: Let him know you realize he has and always will have a life that is separate from your relationship. He'll appreciate hearing it—and being reminded that you have a separate life, too. Right now his divorce and his parenting responsibilities may make excessive demands on his time. Later his own interests and friends will take him away from you now and then. That's something that his soon-to-be-ex wife will have to accept, too. He doesn't have to tell her about you if he doesn't want to. He isn't at her beck and call, and it has nothing to do with whether there's a woman in his life. The same principle applies: He has a right to his own life.

HIS ATTACHMENT TO YOU SOMETIMES FEELS SUFFOCATING

Erika, thirty-seven, met thirty-three-year-old Jon on a blind date in late October. Jon had been separated for several months following an eleven-year marriage. It was love at first sight on both sides, a sweet and immediate soulful connection plus a powerful sexual attraction. "We spent all our free time together, couldn't get enough of each other," says Erika. "We were both neglecting other responsibilities, just enjoying the feelings. Then I pulled away a little—not because I felt less but other obligations became pressing. As soon as I pulled away, there was a change. He was hurt. Then at Christmas we went to a party given by friends of mine, and he accused me of flirting with another man. We had a terrible argument. He called me all the time, always wanting an account of where I'd been, who I'd been with. If I bristled at any of this, he backed down and apologized and said he was just so in love with me, but it started to take a toll on the romance. I had such high hopes for us, but at that point I didn't know whether we'd make it. His ongoing divorce was actually less of a problem than his neediness. I worried that he was neglecting his daughter and not paying enough attention to his work. I loved him, but it was all too much."

Myth: If he's too possessive, get out now. It's only going to escalate.

Reality: You don't have to throw him away if he has become obsessive, but you do have to recognize his neediness, let him know that you're not his savior, and refrain from getting caught up in his drama.

Insight: If either one of you is obsessing, you're in trouble.

Action: Share with him your observation that his attachment to you is particularly powerful. Help him realize that his relationship with you seems to have unlocked strong feelings. Suggest that the two of you take a break. That will break the cycle of his neediness and give you both new perspective.

Silver Lining: Resolve this emotional gridlock, and the two of you can claim an important relationship victory as well as a blueprint for resolving future conflict.

THE TWO OF YOU SPEND MOST OF YOUR TIME TOGETHER IN BED

Sharon and Arthur, both thirty-eight, had known each other casually in college, then gone separate ways, both marrying and starting families outside of Boston. When Sharon's nine-year marriage ended, all she wanted to do was raise her son and rejuvenate a freelance career as a book illustrator. "My marriage had been sexually dead for a long time even before the divorce. I'd lost track of myself sexually. I'd been disconnected from that side of myself for so long that, frankly, I didn't even miss it." Then she met Arthur. "We ran into each other—in Home Depot of all places—shortly after he moved out of his house. His wife had asked for the divorce—she was in love with another man. I have to say, there was an immediate spark. Arthur asked me if I'd like to meet for coffee later in the week, and that's how it started." Their love affair was a sexual revolution for both of them. "Granted we were both sexually starving, but there was a genuine erotic fit between us. We spent all our time together in bed." Sharon felt herself imagining a future with Arthur. But did he feel the same? "He said he was falling in love with me, too. But we had a hard time experiencing each other other than sexually. His time was limited, so was mine. We'd been seeing each other for over a month and hadn't even gone to a movie together. I was worried about where this relationship was going."

Myth: Worrying whether he just loves you for your body is old-fashioned.

Reality: Most relationships start out sexually hot. But if you're thinking about a potential future with this man, you need to know if your relationship satisfies you on other levels, too.

Insight: Am I brave enough to see if this relationship is enough for me? If you are, you have to make it happen.

Action: Don't always have sex when he wants it. Beg off. Tell him you're not in the mood, in a good place for sex tonight. (If your own willpower is overcooked spaghetti, have sex with yourself before you see him.) What's his response to a lustless evening? Is he checking his watch, retreating into sullen silence, or happily cuddling up for a night of companionship and videos?

Silver Lining: Does your relationship have legs? Now's your chance—while you're still hot for each other—to find out how compatible a relationship you actually have.

HIS FINANCIAL BEHAVIOR
WORRIES YOU

Cassie, a dark-haired headhunter in her early thirties, had just broken off a long-term relationship when she fell in love with Doug, a forty-year-old hospital administrator, recently separated and new to Los Angeles. Doug was torn at having to live at a distance from his eight-year-old son. He had moved to take advantage of a job opportunity he felt he couldn't afford to pass up, especially now that he had two households to support. "Every other weekend Doug flew back to Chicago to see his son," says Cassie. "That was tough on him, but his guilt was causing him to lavish the kid with presents because he couldn't be there all the time. I understood his motivation, but it seemed misguided to me. Also, his wife was demanding a financial arrangement that really drained him. I admit it was tough for me to see him support this woman who'd never held a job in her life. I wait-

ressed all through college, and I've been self-supporting ever since. I was critical of Doug for giving in to those demands. It wasn't just sour grapes. He'd complain about his money problems, then he'd be extravagant with me, too. We were falling in love, but I felt concerned about his financial behavior. We talked about having children of our own. Didn't he realize that he was going to be supporting two families?"

Myth: In order to stay out of his financial negotiations and settlement, you must keep silent about how you see his financial behavior.

Reality: His divorce settlement is one thing. His feelings and behavior are another. You can help him distinguish his obligations to his family from his guilty feelings. You can help him see how he acts out that conflict through money.

Insight: Acknowledge your own prejudices, too. Cassie's resentment of Doug's wife is understandable, but for Cassie to act out of that resentment or encourage Doug to share such feelings could only harm their developing relationship. If you're terribly disappointed that your boyfriend isn't spending a lot of money on you, better ask yourself what you're in this relationship for. Is he really the man you want? Betsy, a thirty-nine-year-old hat designer, is involved with a man whose money style was forged during the financially flush days of his marriage. His business is shakier these days, and his impending divorce is financially strapping. "But he still lives as if he's got all the money in the world, and that worries me," she says. "He's a wonderful, caring man, but it scares me to think how his spending could affect our future together. I make a real effort not to nag him. I ask him if he's interested in my observations, and then I tell him that I'm concerned. I know he'll be successful again, but I also let him know that his readiness to indulge himself and his kids right now is worrisome."

Action: Encourage your man to spend time with his children *and* to be aware that overspending on his part might well be an attempt to make up for the past. Be consistent with your own expectations. If he has money problems, encourage him to not overspend on you, either.

Silver Lining: Developing respect for money as a couple is part of the foundation you create for a future partnership.

FRIENDS DISAPPROVE OF YOUR RELATIONSHIP

When Tammy, a twenty-seven-year-old airline employee, fell in love with thirty-three-year-old Ken, a high school teacher who'd left his marriage after a year and a half, she couldn't wait to tell her friends and family all about the tall, soft-spoken scientist who loved cats and kids and hid his sly sense of humor behind a disarming shyness. "Everyone I'm close to was horrified," says Tammy. "I wanted to share my happiness and their reaction was, he's on the rebound, he must be really messed-up, you're going to get your heart broken. That hurt." Some of Ken's friends also disapproved of the relationship. "His two good female friends were especially disapproving. True, he hadn't been married long, but it's not as if I stole him from his wife! They seemed to expect him to go through a period of celibacy before he was 'allowed' to date. That was the general consensus: take a year off. How is it that everyone gives that advice? Love doesn't make an appointment! Were we supposed to turn away from this wonderful connection just because the timing didn't seem right to everyone else?"

Myth: Your friends can be objective.

Reality: Most friends will be anything but objective. It's the rare friend or family member who can resist projecting their own fears and desires onto your romantic situation. However, friends and family do know *you*. If they're just about unanimous in their response to your boyfriend's behavior, pay attention. They can't always know your tolerance, but they do know who you are. If they really don't like the guy, pay attention.

Insight: Despite the fact that your boyfriend is separated, some of your friends will be tempted to see you as having an affair with a married man and will disapprove.

Action: Lean on this book for advice. Factor in the responses from family and friends who know you well, and treasure that one friend who really lets you express your own feelings. Consider seeing a therapist, a minister, a rabbi. Don't turn to friends and/or family who can't support you in the ways you need to be supported. They want to protect you, but they can only give you advice based on their own experience.

Silver Lining: This cliché holds true: When you survive an emotional crisis, you discover who your friends are. And you discover your own strengths and capacity for growth.

And always—remember your three options:

● You can bail out of the relationship.

● You can put the relationship on hold.

● You can continue with the relationship.

DR. LESLIE PAM'S CHAPTER CHECKPOINTS

1. It's your responsibility to recognize the difference between your old need patterns and your present-day need patterns. If you're upset because he seems to be rejecting you, not giving you what you want, ask yourself if you've been here before. Are these feelings familiar? Are you recreating an old scenario? Admit you're confused. Run a reality check with friends who know you well.

2. Is the balance between you fair? Your life—your friends, work, parents, vacation times—makes as many demands on your time as his divorce, children, and wife do on him.

Does he always expect you to capitulate when there's a conflict, or is there a balance? If the balance is off, let him know. When he's out of line, does he respond with a desire to right the balance, or is he cranky and defensive?

3. Tell him what you need. Keep sharing your feelings and thoughts. If you hold back feelings, assuming he knows how you feel, and nurture small grievances you will surely be misunderstood. Start from the assumption that he misunderstands you, and then try to make yourself understood. Good relationships don't censor negative feelings, they develop smart strategies for dealing with them. Use these misunderstandings as an opportunity to create relationship rules and boundaries.

4. Make sure the relationship rules apply to both of you. If he has the luxury of canceling a date because of a last-minute family crisis, does he afford you the same luxury? Can you take advantage of that luxury? Try not to get stuck in hurt feelings. Speak up, and get past the hurt.

5. Play out small grievances in your head before having the confrontation with him. What will you say? What will he say? What do you imagine the outcome will be? Are you jumping to a conclusion that's unrealistic? Maybe you don't have to have this particular confrontation. Don't do things when you're angry.

CHAPTER EIGHT

Will You Be the Transitional Woman?

For Valentine's Day, he bought her a heart-shaped pin made of tiny little rubies. "You are my jewel, you own my heart," the card said. On her birthday he took her to Sun Valley, where snow flakes sparkled like diamonds in her blonde hair and he teased her, calling her his ski angel. "You've changed my life, you are my happiness," he whispered as they snuggled before the fire. She had never been so much in love. When she spoke their two names aloud—Valerie and Marvin, Valerie and Marvin—the sound they made felt like musical notes to her ear (an ear that now sported a perfect diamond stud, "just for being you."). Their names made magic; they were the sound of fate speaking up for itself.

Her friends were getting a little bit sick of it. It wasn't simply that the man wasn't divorced. That was bad enough. But he canceled dates with Valerie and took her outrageously for granted. He screamed at his wife, whom he insisted was an insane person, right in front of her! He turned their lovely, frisky friend Valerie into a doormat, albeit a bejeweled doormat. She kept a cell phone strapped to her person in case he called. She was never available anymore for dinners and fun, her Filofax was blank for the possibility of all-Marvin, all the time. She began to talk of moving to the city where he spent most of his bicoastal time. "He's a maniac," they suggested. "He's obnoxious," they hinted. "He'll never get divorced, it's all about the money," they implied.

Her therapist, frankly concerned, tried metaphor therapy.

"Imagine that for the next year or so you're hanging onto a rope that's attached to the back of a speeding motorboat. That motorboat is racing across some very choppy water, picking up speed, and your hands are getting chafed and bloodied. You might want to let go and have the boat come back and get you.

"Or imagine that Marvin is the king of a country engaged in a brutal and horrible war. The two of you can escape to a beautiful island, off the coast of that country, but Marvin spends so much time in that war zone, where the shrapnel flies and bombs explode, that you want to be with him there as well. Eventually he associates you with the war zone and not the paradise."

But Valerie quit her job. She moved to the war zone. She clutched the rope more tightly. She rubbed Marvin's back and massaged his temples with eucalyptus oil when his wife made his head pound. Months went by, and still Marvin wasn't hers. Valerie became somewhat less angelic. She demanded to see his attorneys. She demanded to see his wife. She demanded to see her engagement ring—*now!*

One day Marvin came home and took Valerie in his arms. "I have an idea," he said. "Well, to give credit where it's due, it was my wife's idea. She suggested we just stay separated, never get divorced, but lead separate lives. What do you think?"

His blonde angel, the love of his life, his happiness, didn't think much of it.

Today Marvin is a bad memory with some nice jewelry. And Valerie admits: "I did everything wrong. I went from being a loving, sweet, reasonable woman to being a wreck. I let him and his divorce turn me inside out. I waited for a single act, a solitary deci-sion—a divorce decree or a marriage proposal—to change every-thing, to define my entire future."

Do you still believe that the decision to spend a lifetime with him will happen in one magical moment—A signature across a legal document? A diamond ring winking up from the bottom of the soufflé dish? When the two of you, enfolded in each other's arms, finally know *This Is It*?

But the decision to make that mutual commitment actually evolves slowly, out of hundreds of small, everyday exchanges tak-ing place between you and him, you and yourself, you and the outside world. Together these changes prepare head and heart for love in general and a commitment to that lovable and less-than-perfect person in particular.

If readiness for commitment doesn't strike like lightning—he signs his divorce papers, then falls to his knees—how will you know when it's arrived? How will you know that this love affair isn't destined to be a transitional relationship? Is there anything you can do to safeguard your relationship right now, today, so that it isn't that passing love affair, so that it does continue to acquire the momentum necessary for a real and long-lasting commitment?

We know it's your biggest fear, the scenario everyone's warned you about, the flip side of your gratefulness for having met this wonderful man you love so much before some other lucky woman got there first. The worry stalks you: Was your timing so terrific after all? After everything you've been through with this man, will you wind up being his rebound woman, his post-divorce love affair, the nurse-him-back-to-mental-health sweetheart who suf-fers with him through the excruciatingly boring agonies of his divorce, his low self-esteem, and his questionable testosterone level, then gets dumped along with the crummy bachelor apart-ment and the attorney, the woman who patiently whips him into shape for a genuine, loving, adult relationship, the woman who spent eight hours playing cat's cradle with his whiny daughter and watching *Rugrats* with his son, the woman who taught him everything he knows about how to love and how to dress, the woman whose heart he apologizes for breaking just before moving on to his one true, lasting, happily-ever-after love? Will you be his transitional girlfriend?

Yes, you probably will.

Have we ever lied to you? Didn't we tell you it was a high-risk relationship? Did you forget?

Get hold of yourself. The operative word here is "probably". You *can* lower the risks. That's the point. It has always been the point. Are you still willing to do everything you can to lower the risks in your favor, to avoid being the transitional woman?

Good. Now we're going to tell you how.

ASSUME YOU ARE THE TRANSITIONAL WOMAN

That's right. Just assume it right now. Yes, we understand that you've spent all your adult life telling yourself that you can have what you want (hello, Oprah). Yes, you are a beautiful, loving, accomplished woman who sees the glass as half-full, who visualizes success and goes for it, whose inner warrior goddess brims with confidence, pluck, and just the right amount of bravado.

Now we're telling you to look in the mirror and throw cold water in your face. Tell yourself: Just because he's divorcing his wife doesn't mean he's going to end up with me.

Starry-eyed and romantic isn't going to win the day. Angry and determined not to let him take an iota of advantage of your healthy, stand-up-for-your-rights self isn't going to win the day. Realism does win the day. And the realist says to herself: "Okay, winding up together is not an outcome with the highest probability." Then she shrugs and takes her best shot, using every ounce of love smarts she can muster. Assuming that clear-eyed, negative outcome isn't defeatist. It's more about giving yourself a floor, a net, a bottom-line reminder that every time you get too comfy with how it's all going to turn out is exactly the time to pull yourself up short and remember the high-risk enterprise you're engaged in to begin with.

RATCHET DOWN YOUR REQUIREMENTS

This might sound counterintuitive, but it's really not. When you were twenty, you had approximately three requirements for the man who would win your heart. Now that you're older and wiser, you have about three hundred, right? You've learned through hard experience exactly what you will and will not tolerate in a relationship.

Well, now we're telling you to let those requirements go. Rip up that list and throw it in the garbage. Along with the list of requirements, trash the anger and the righteous indignation lurking between the lines. Drop the "show-me" attitude.

When you embark upon a relationship with requirements, this is what your beloved hears you saying: "Hey, buddy. You have to be someone other than who you are. I don't accept you the way you are."

The flawed if hunky lunk you fell in love with is not going to meet your list of requirements. Count on it. And the woman who gets cast as transitional girlfriend is the woman who isn't smart enough to recognize that personality and events are fluid—and will change as situations move forward. She's stuck in her idea of how a relationship should be.

"I met Mark during the year of his divorce," says Amy, a forty-eight-year-old independent film producer. "When we met, he said, 'I'm getting a divorce, I have two kids, and I definitely don't want more kids. I don't even know if I want to get married again.' I told him that I didn't even know if I wanted to see him next Saturday night, let alone marry him and have his children! Inwardly, though, I was conscious of choosing to take a huge risk. I did want children in my life, and I definitely wanted a marriage." Amy and Mark continued to see each other. "I decided that as long as Mark and I were enjoying each other, I would wait and see. He had so many qualities I loved, and we had such a wonderful time together." After Mark's divorce became final, Amy and Mark had another conversation about the future. "He told me that, though he wasn't absolutely ruling marriage out, he needed to feel and be divorced first. It's not that he wanted to date around—we were definitely seeing each other exclusively—but he wasn't ready to even consider marriage. Marriage to him was the equivalent of divorce, emotionally. Why would he want to risk that again? As for children? He wasn't at all ambivalent on that score. Been there, done that. He knew he didn't want to be back in parenthood again." Again, Amy made a choice: Wait and see.

"Another woman might have walked, but I knew I'd found a terrific guy. I could consider revising my expectations." Which is what she did. After they'd been seeing each other for eighteen months, Mark moved into Amy's apartment. Three years later, they married. "I willingly, if reluctantly, gave up the possibility of motherhood. But I'm a stepmother to Mark's two kids, whom I adore, and I feel fortunate to have those relationships. Not to mention the fact that I have a wonderful marriage. Mark couldn't give me everything I wanted, but I have most of it. I'm a happy woman. We each helped the other remain open to possibilities for happiness we hadn't considered."

Maybe you feel differently. If you're dating a divorcing man with kids who has expressed an unwillingness to have more children or an ambivalence, and children are your heart's desire, real-ize that you might be taking a big risk. On the other hand, a man in the midst of a divorce is unlikely to embrace the concept of more children to theoretically disappoint, support, lose. Listen to what he's saying and respect his views, but if you're hell-bent on kids wait until the dust settles—or cut your losses now.

ACKNOWLEDGE THE POWER OF THE TRIANGLE

Thirty-four-year-old Angela is a home furnishings buyer for a large Southern department store chain. At twenty-three, Angela had an affair with a married man, but as soon as his marriage ended, Angela ended the relationship, concerned that there was too big an age difference between them. At thirty, Angela fell in love with a single man who left her twice—both times for a woman he'd been involved with when Angela met him. "I proba-bly should have learned my lesson the first time, but I gave it a sec-ond try." It took her two years to recover from that heartbreak. Now she's dating Billy, a colleague who has been separated from his wife for a little over a year. "I'm hoping to make this relation-ship work," says Angela. "Billy is a great guy, and his marriage is definitely over. Right now, he's fighting with his wife over the financial settlement. And I'm fighting with my past. I don't want this love affair to disappoint me the way the others did." Angela is aware that her romantic history has most often involved a trian-gle—a love affair in which there was always another woman involved somewhere in the shadows. Angela is drawn to triangles and recognizes that behavior in herself. "I'm trying to break the pattern," she admits.

Triangles can exert an almost magical pull over our love lives. The reasons lie in the past when, as little girls, we were learning from both our parents what it meant to be a woman and how to go about claiming the attention of a man. Every one of us remains in thrall to the built-in disappointment of the triangle—after all, as children we were ill-equipped to win our first and earliest love. That's the way it's supposed to be. We grow up to find a new love, one of our own. That emotional evolution is part of the complex psychology of early family life. But that earliest erotic and emotional imprinting can turn out to be more powerful and more potentially hurtful in the adult lives of some women than in others. Angela's parents had an embattled marriage in which her father, after a series of infidelities, finally left the marriage. Angela saw her mother as inadequate and unloved. In her adult love affairs, Angela is time after time compelled to reenact that early triangle, to compete with another woman to prove her own desirability. She's compelled to become that other woman of her childhood.

When we don't consciously understand and attempt to heal childhood disappointments and injuries—incest, abandonment, or emotional and physical abuse—we may not acquire the self-respect needed to protect ourselves from painful love as grown women. This isn't about being a "good" woman or a "bad" woman. We're all products of our childhoods, one way or another. But as grown women we have choices about how we want to live our lives. We can choose to be emotional archaeologists, looking in our present-day love affairs for clues to our pasts. Like Angela, we can choose to struggle with those early psychic losses and triumph over them. "Every one of those love affairs felt destined to me," says Angela now. "They all felt familiar and right. I didn't realize it was because they shared the same emotional themes that I knew as a kid. Now I realize they were choosing me."

If you suspect that, like Angela, you're a woman with a weakness for triangles, it's in your interest to recognize that vulnerability. Does it mean you're "wrong" to have fallen in love with a man who isn't completely free of his marriage? No. But it does mean you have to be careful to avoid a destructive outcome.

Listen to yourself. If you hear yourself saying, "This time is different," consider it a sign you've fallen under the spell! Remind yourself instead that this time is the same.

Then ask yourself: "What can I do to make sure the *outcome* will be different this time?"

PICK YOUR BATTLES

One way to change the outcome is to know which relationship battles are worth fighting and which aren't.

Not worth fighting	Instead
You hate how his kids behave.	Be scarce when they're around. If you're with him when they misbehave, take him aside and tell him you're uncomfortable.
His wife makes outrageous demands.	Try telling him that you know he'll handle it as best he can with his attorney. Then go to a yoga class.
You don't spend enough time socializing as a couple.	See your friends on your own until the dust of his divorce clears.
He doesn't want to plan next winter's vacation with you.	Realize you're still on Divorce Time. Postpone those plans, or take a trip on your own.

Worth fighting	How to fight it
He's always complaining about his: career, money problems, kids.	Say, "I've been hearing this same story for a long time. I need to know what it is you want. Do you just want me to listen and be sympathetic, or do you want me to help you move forward? Because I'm getting a little bogged down by this story."
He promises to carve out time for the two of you, but it doesn't happen.	Say, "I appreciate that our relationship can't be all it should be right now, but if we can't be together it can't be a relationship at all. If you can't find time for me, let's decide together to put it on hold until we can both give it what it needs to flourish."
He doesn't give you clear information about where his divorce stands.	Tell him you don't need the blow-by-blow details, but you want the big picture. Why is he unable to share it? Is he unclear himself? If you're unsure if he and his wife have filed papers, you can check public records at the county courthouse.

BE MORE REAL THAN HONEST

Don't just tell him about yourself: *Be yourself.* Chances are you have a few ideas of your own about marriage and divorce and infidelity and kids and working women and parenting and how a healthy relationship ought to operate. Well, he probably doesn't want to hear about it. If you don't want to be the transitional woman, stop acting as if every date is another stop on the campaign trail in disguise. Stop stumping for the role of Second Wife. Stop making claims about what you will and will not tolerate In a Relationship. Refrain from holding forth about how you are Different From All Other Women; Most Specifically, His Wife. Frankly, men don't want that much conversation. They just want a real woman. Don't tell him you're Honest, Independent, and Healthy. Just go ahead and be that woman.

Patricia met Victor when he moved into her apartment complex a few months after filing for divorce. "Victor needed a girlfriend who was willing to just echo his anger at his wife," says Patricia. "I couldn't do that. He'd tell me stories about his marriage and about their ongoing divorce and sometimes I'd feel, well your wife has a point, and I'd tell him why I thought so. I supported Victor, I was always on his side, but sometimes I really did see his wife's point of view. Especially as I got to know him better. So I'd tell him what I thought. I said, "I have no bone to pick with this woman. Let your attorney be outraged on your behalf." When Victor fell in love with Patricia, he might have thought he needed a yes-woman. What he got was a real woman. And his love affair with her continues.

SEE THE OUTCOME AS YOUR DECISION

Have you turned into the Human Female Relationship Richter Scale? Every time your love affair suffers a tremor or a quake—he temporarily pulls away or sinks into confusion or ambivalence or worse—have you no sooner rated the psychic damage than you're back to work rebuilding the relationship?

Stop trying so hard!

The woman destined to be transitional is the woman who thinks it's up to *him* to make the decision. She makes the mistake of thinking she knows what he wants, and he doesn't. She mis-reads the signals. When he pulls back, she moves closer. Her need-iness causes her to interpret his distance as an invitation to work harder to get him.

No, no, no! You must refuse to be that woman! You must see this love affair as your decision.

How do you do that? Especially when his behavior really does leave you feeling rejected, insecure, and a tad panicky?

Katherine, forty, a massage therapist and healer, dated Stan immediately following his separation. "Stan was so cautious he couldn't express a single loving emotion without in some way qualifying it for fear I'd get the wrong idea about his availability," she says. "I just refused to be the cheerleader for the relationship. It's what women are always doing—I've done it myself more times than I can say. I made a point of letting Stan know that I had my own doubts about getting close. I also told him that I wanted to be very careful not to get involved with a man who really was inca-pable of making a commitment. I told him that I didn't see shar-ing my life with someone who couldn't make that leap of faith. That kind of conversation with Stan, where we were each airing our uncertainties, felt a lot different than those conversations with men who are pulling away while your heart is sinking into your stomach."

Recognize what Katherine recognized: most people have trou-ble knowing what they want. Don't you?

BE BOLD

Anya, thirty-eight, a costume designer, first met forty-four-year-old Jeremy, a restaurateur, at an Alcoholics Anonymous meeting in Los Angeles. "I was in L.A. for work, stopped in at a meeting, and was introduced to him briefly afterwards by a mutual friend," she says. "I couldn't get his face—especially his eyes, which were this incredibly intense blue-green—out of my mind for days. All my friends knew was that he was married. I forgot about him." Close to a year later, Anya and Jeremy found each other by chance in the same elevator in a New York City apartment building. "We remembered each other instantly, and this time there was a spark. We were both leaving the building—we'd been visiting friends—and went for coffee together." Jeremy, newly separated from his wife, had moved to the city. He and Anya began dating. They fell in love. "This relationship felt like kismet from the start. I mean, what are the chances that we'd ever meet again? Even through all our setbacks, I felt emboldened to stick with it. I thought we were really destined to be together."

Anya's faith was tested over the next year. Jeremy had two children, whom he visited regularly in L.A. During one of those visits, his wife told him that she had breast cancer. "He was devastated," says Anya. "She went through surgery and chemo, and the divorce proceedings were put on hold. Jeremy moved back to care for the kids. He was torn by guilt, as if he'd brought on the cancer." Another year went by. "Our relationship was long distance, which was hard enough. Plus his wife was ill, he felt responsible. I had a hard time asking for much. I saw other men during that year, but I was pretty much going through the motions. I really loved this guy."

Two days after Jeremy's wife was found to be on the road to recovery, Anya packed her bags, flew to Los Angeles, and proposed to the man she loved. "I arranged a romantic evening, looked gorgeous, set the scene, popped the question. I felt I had to bring things to a head. I was ready to marry him or walk. Sitting there at dinner, in this wonderful candlelit garden, it was the last thing he expected to hear, believe me. But I knew I didn't have it in me to not know any longer. I was prepared to leave that restaurant, if necessary, with a broken heart and never turn back. So I told him how much I loved him and how much I wanted to live my life loving him. And I asked him, just like in the movies, if he would

marry me. And I guess he was just too overcome to even equivo-
cate. And he said yes."

Do you have it in you to try something that bold and romantic?
Make a gesture so grand and irrevocable that, whatever your outcome, he'll never forget you.

GET A (PLAN B) ROMANTIC LIFE

Yes, you need a rich, full life—a life that you can sink into like a
big fluffy down comforter on a wintry evening or plunge into like
an icy pool on a sultry day. But beyond friends, activities, and
family, you also need the potential for alternative romance if you
intend to survive his divorce with your womanly ego and emotional equilibrium intact. Here's a paradox about that often pitiful
creature, the divorcing man, we've been describing to you: He's
already got that alternative love life. He has a family. Yes, maybe it's
miserable, but it's still there. As an unattached woman, you don't
have that emotional fallback, that psychic net for the down days
and the existential I'm-all-alone-in-the-world and what's-it-all-
about-anyway moments. That's why you need that fully function-
ing backdrop, romantic interest and all, that you can summon up
when necessary. Of course you will be tempted, in the first exhil-
arating days of romance, to abandon your wonderful friends, your
rich and complex life. That's natural. Of course the thought of
another man leaves you cold. Fine. Do it anyway. Go through the
motions. It's psychic protection. Abandon your life or your own
romantic potential, and you leave yourself wide open for being
that transitional woman.

More than your book club, the gym, your three best friends, and
Thanksgiving at your mother's house, you need to know that if
this love affair doesn't work out, you will live to love again. You
need to remind yourself that other men find you adorable and
desirable. (Do you find any of those men adorable or desirable?

This is totally beside the point, believe us.) Men waiting in the wings of your life are psychological armor for the dark days. What do you think you're going to be doing when the two of you decide to take a break, when you tell him you have to step away until something changes, when he is so enmeshed with his kids and his wife there's not time for you? You're going to be dating! Even if that means going through the motions of dating. You didn't think you were going to spend those Saturday nights watching *Xena: Warrior Princess*, did you?

Stephanie, forty-one, had a few almost-but-not-quite romantic possibilities hovering around the edges of her life when she fell in love with fifty-year-old Henry, a marketing executive she met at a sales meeting. "I felt ambivalent about those other men, but Henry and I connected from the start," she says. "We didn't live in the same city, but we had so much to say to each other from the start that we were determined to make it work. We were always laughing, always having the best time. We wanted to be with each other more than anyone else in the world." Except that Henry wasn't yet divorced, and wouldn't be for another two years. "I went through every stage possible in this relationship," says Stephanie. "The long-distance aspect of the relationship was tough, but in a way it helped balance the frustration of waiting for his divorce."

Henry claimed he needed to secure his financial life before he signed off on the divorce. He and his wife had been separated for a year, and they had managed to remain friends, sharing custody of their two sons. "After eight months, I felt fed up with dating a married man. But I loved Henry, and our relationship was great. We managed to see each other often, and we both wanted the relationship to continue. Meeting his kids was a big step—mostly overcoming Henry's anxieties about how they'd react to a woman in his life. The kids were fine. But still the divorce wasn't happening." According to Stephanie, the key to managing her frustration with Henry—and protecting the relationship—was reminding herself that she had other romantic options.

138 How to Survive Your Boyfriend's Divorce

"A year into our relationship—that was two years into Henry's separation—I simply became more vocal and determined about my expectations," says Stephanie. "I was willing to say, I can't wait until the last minute to know whether we'll be together on a holiday. Or, if we're a couple then we can decide together about how to deal with the kids. Or just reminding him that I never signed on to be with a married man forever. Whenever I felt that he was taking advantage of my patience, I let him know that the message I was getting was that we weren't on the same page about what this relationship meant." Stephanie stepped away from the relationship several times. "Granted, that was easier to do in a long-distance romance, but I would have done it anyway. And every time I stepped back, I made sure I had a date with someone else. Every time I started feeling needy, I made a date with someone else. I had two men in my life who'd been interested in me for a while. I wasn't sexually intimate with either one, but I did go out and have fun. It's amazing how little it takes to restore your perspective. I didn't sit around and sulk over Henry. I wouldn't allow myself to do it. I felt like I was running a marathon and needed to pace myself. Those dates were my version of water stops. They renewed my energy and helped give me a second wind. We were together another eight months before Henry divorced and we began to plan our life."

No matter what, you still have the same three options you had from the start:

- You can bail out of the relationship.

- You can put the relationship on hold.

- You can continue with the relationship.

DR. LESLIE PAM'S CHAPTER CHECKPOINTS

1. Beware of being his default relationship. Even when he finally is divorced, you don't want him on those terms. That's not a victory. You want him because he really wants to be with you—or you'll never be sure of him.

2. Is the relationship growing on its own terms? Or is there always an element of "When I get divorced, everything will be different"? This is your relationship, right now.

3. How will you handle him without his wife in the picture? Don't underestimate her role in his life. She has been providing him with something, filling certain needs. Ask yourself what they might be. When the job is 100 percent yours, will you be able to handle him?

4. It's need that's blind, not love. Desperation is the agent that blinds. Love feels good and need hurts—that's how to know which state you're in. If you can identify your neediness, you can't be controlled or manipulated by it.

5. Take his "celebration" temperature. When you want to mark your one-month, three-month, or six-month anniversary together with a celebratory dinner, what's his response?

CHAPTER NINE

Have You Waited Too Long?

ULTIMATUMS, LAST-DITCH STRATEGIES, AND YOUR INVISIBLE LINE

"I don't know if I want to get married again."

The man speaking those words wasn't on a first date, making get-to-know-you, first-date dinner conversation with a woman he barely knew. He was the just-divorced lover of a woman who had waited for eighteen difficult months, through an intense, loving, and committed relationship, to reach this milestone. This celebration dinner—at their favorite candlelit bistro, the scene of their first romantic date—was supposed to mark The End of All That: the end of the waiting, the end of the frustration, the end of the secrecy, the end of the uncertainty. And a new beginning.

"You don't know if you want to get married again?"

It wasn't that she expected a proposal that very night, although she wouldn't have been disappointed in one—not a ring maybe, but a statement of intention, a declaration, an avowal. After all, they'd talked about marriage, about the future, many times. Their shared assumption—of course they would be together, anything else was unthinkable—was what warmed and consoled them through the hard months of his divorce. When they met, through a community association in the neighborhood where they both lived, they had agreed to move slowly. He was just out of his marriage, she was beginning again after a long-term relationship. Still, they fell in love. And all along he'd been amazingly generous with his emotions and his time given the restrictions, the emotional duress, the problems with the kids, and all the other complications inherent in ending one life while beginning another.

It was never a question of whether. It was always a matter of when. It had never occurred to her that, with his divorce at last a fact, he might suddenly step away. Never.

After that night, she went to bed for a week.

When she was cried out, she'd arrived at a new place, carried there by a sea of tears. She stood at the edge of another country, a dangerous place inside herself. She could see that new place from where she now was, still safe. It was across a line, an invisible line. Yet it was a demarcation as precise to her emotional geography as the equator is to the world's physical geography. Across that line was a place in which her love for this man and their bond was a thing of the past. A dead thing. Over. Beyond anger and tears. Beyond doubt and resentment. All she knew was, she didn't want to live in that country. She knew she had to do everything in her power not to cross over that line.

"I respect the fact that you can't consider marriage right now," she told him when she picked herself up off her bed. "I love you and hope you will take all the time you need to make that decision. I'm hoping that marriage is in our future, but for right now I plan to resume my life, the life I had before you. I still want you in it, just not so solidly in the dead-center of it." Then she went horseback riding for two weeks. When she returned, she felt a renewed energy for life. She decided to learn how to play the piano. She joined a book club. She began keeping a journal. She reconnected with old friends and made new ones. One or two of them were men she saw for dinner and movies, men she thought about kissing. She saw him, too. Lovingly. Sweetly. Passionately.

But something had changed. "For the first time in a long long time, I really liked my life," she said. "I wasn't waiting for something to happen. I felt happy and complete."

Three months later, he proposed.

"I really don't think I want to get married right now," she told him. Amazingly, she meant it.

He asked again five months later, then again eight months later. (Because even more amazingly, the change in her had sparked a responsive change in him.) This time she accepted.

A full year after that terrible week spent sobbing across her bed, the two of them planned their wedding—and, happily, became husband and wife.

YOUR INVISIBLE LINE

There's an invisible line inside the heart. On one side of that line is hope. On the other side is the death of hope. On one side of that line is love. On the other side is indifference, the death of love. When you cross that line within yourself, your love affair becomes unrevivable. Anger has poisoned it. Disappointment has smothered it. Promises made and broken have crippled it. On one side of the line is your healthy desire to compromise, negotiate, understand, endure, and triumph. On the other side is the unhealthy obsession with a relationship that has taken on a negative life of its own and swept you up in the day-to-day pain of living inside that negative reality, inside the negation of your own happiness and well-being, the muting of your own true voice, the selling out of your heart's desire.

You don't want to cross that invisible line.

At the start of this book we compared falling in love with a divorcing man to climbing Mt. Everest. We cautioned that you were taking on a big risk, the outcome highly uncertain. Not a normal dating-and-maybe-falling-in-love risk—a bigger risk. We suggested that you ask yourself if you were the kind of woman who *could* take such a risk. Based on all the available information you had then, and probably a healthy leap of faith, you decided you were. We applaud your brave heart. You would control what was in your power to control—your physical condition, your supplies and gear, your teammates, and the right time for the ascent in terms of weather conditions. And that's what you did.

But now that you've climbed over two-thirds of the way to the top, you see that despite your best weather predictions a fierce storm is gathering. It's snowing heavily, and the winds are picking up. Worse, your clothing isn't keeping you warm—you're chilled to the bone and wet. Your supplies are running out.

What do you do?

Do you keep climbing?

Or do you descend to a safer place on the mountain, where the storm isn't howling and where, after some rest and a change of clothes, you might get a better picture of the situation?

Or do you even return to base camp, feeling lucky to get out with your life even if the whole expedition wound up a bust?

Probably by now you've been through some tough, painful times. Certainly you've learned some things about yourself, about him, about relationships, about love. If you're lucky, the two of you have formed a solid bond, have learned something about negotiating your differences, have fought and made up and then some—and you're still together. The stress and the pressure surrounding your relationship have perhaps uncovered more than you ever thought you wanted to know about your own and his vulnerabilities and flaws—but all you need to know about your own and his capacity for love, for generosity, for understanding. You still love him. He still loves you. You both continue to believe you're a great team.

There's only one obstacle standing in the way of your happiness: He's still not divorced.

Or, he is divorced, but he doesn't know what he wants.

Are We There Yet?

"Michael and I had been dating for three years—his divorce had dragged on for close to four—and on the weekends we'd drive through different neighborhoods to look at houses we imagined some day buying together," says fifty-eight-year-old Janet. "One Sunday we stopped in at an open house and took the house tour. The realtor asked us if he needed rooms for grandchildren. Michael was sixty, so naturally we looked the part of a long-married couple. At that moment, I began to feel dizzy—literally. And nauseated. I felt like a child caught out in some naughty game of pretend. What was I doing? After everything we'd been through . . . and still his divorce hadn't happened. That was the moment I crossed over a line inside myself. I practically ran out of that house. I'd had it."

How do you know when you're approaching your invisible line? Just last week or last month or last year, when you felt most in love with him, you knew his divorce would happen. You were in it with him, willing to see it through. So what's changed? Nothing—and everything. What was bearable (even if only just-bearable) is now decidedly not.

What happened?

For some women, the signal is as clear and unequivocal as Janet's wave of dizziness. Standing there, dizzy and ashamed, she knew she was out of patience. She was no longer willing to live her life "as if." That feeling was her signal to herself that the status quo would no longer do. That weekend, Janet made a decision to step away from the relationship that had become the center of her life. She sensed for the first time that her feelings for this man were about to shift "I felt like I was at the edge of an emotional abyss," she says. "If I didn't step away I was going to end up feeling contempt for him. I didn't want to do that. I waited a few days, thinking that this new sense of things would pass, the way feelings often do, but they didn't." Janet told him how she felt. "I said that if we continued as we were, the relationship was going to be damaged. My resentment was eroding the feeling. I supposed I could have said the same thing just to manipulate him, but I don't think it would have had the same effect. You can't fake a real conviction, a real feeling. He could tell I was serious, and that he could lose me. I told him I wanted him to do whatever he had to do, that I still cared for him, that I'd be ready to reconsider the relationship when his divorce papers were signed. And then I stuck to my guns. I'm not saying I didn't miss him—I did. It was painful to withdraw like that. But I knew that every day I'd get a little stronger. And I knew that he was missing me. I counted on it. He called me a few times, and I was warm but restrained. Three months later, he managed to sign those divorce papers."

Your wake-up call may not be as clear as Janet's. (Probably you've pressed the snooze alarm on that wake-up call more times than you can count.) That's why you have to pay even more attention to patterns of thought and behavior that will warn you when you're getting close.

Consider your invisible line the equivalent of a two-month warning. Believe that that's how long your love affair has if you cross it.

On one side of that line, you still have a lot of choices about how to proceed.

On the other side, you put your relationship on death row.

When you cross that invisible line, you give up yourself. You misstate selling out your soul for compromise. You choose him over yourself. And inevitably, you lose both.

Six Signs You've Reached Your Invisible Line

1. You're more concerned about him and what he needs than you are about yourself.

Marlene, a large, lush-figured blonde with a big voice and a ready laugh, is a marketing executive who vibrates with confidence. She and her boyfriend Daniel, a theater designer, had been navigating the drama of his divorce for close to two years. Marlene is no one's idea of a pushover, not in love or anywhere else. She's a spirited (some would say bossy) woman. Marlene had opinions, advice, a point of view about Daniel's parenting skills, his son's difficulties in schools, his wife's lawyers' tactics, Daniel's reluctance to see to his own physical well-being by failing to keep a regular workout schedule, Daniel's therapist and his therapist's analysis of Daniel's relationship with his wife, his children, and Marlene.

And Marlene herself? Her friends and family wondered where she'd disappeared to. Her life's work had become Daniel: supporting him, advising him, anticipating him. You'd never mistake Marlene for a submissive or subservient girlfriend. It wasn't that. It was more a matter of having slowly slipped into Daniel's skin. She was living his life as him as well as with him. When Marlene rejected out-of-hand an opportunity to accept a challenging new job she'd been headhunted for because it would involve too much time away from Daniel, friends became concerned. They told her they thought she was in trouble.

"I was the last to know," Marlene says now. "I have never thought of myself as a love-too-much kind of woman, someone who'd lose or degrade herself for a man. Now I see that my energetic efforts to take the reins of Daniel's life was a poor substitute for everything I couldn't have—building a real life with him." She was walking the invisible line when friends persuaded her to step back and take a look at where she was. She did. Now she says it saved her relationship. "I was doing my best to ignore my own resentment. The angrier I felt, the more I tried to insinuate myself into Daniel's life. Eventually, that anger and resentment would have killed my feelings for him, period."

She told him she felt they needed some time apart. It wound up being six months. "They were tough—we didn't see each other at all. By the end of that time, he was divorced. I felt bruised, still. I was definitely more in touch with my anger and resentment. But we began dating, very gingerly. And something very interesting happened. I began to wonder if I even wanted to marry Daniel. Now that he was divorced, it was a brand-new relationship." It took another year for this couple to arrive at a decision to marry. "We started over. Which is where we are now, and more in love than ever."

How does an otherwise feisty, self-loving woman begin to lose track of herself? This is not some weird and utterly unthinkable phenomenon, like an asteroid just happening to barrel out of the sky to strike the exact Starbucks where you just happen to be in line waiting for your café mocha. It's practically unavoidable. It's the direct result of his divorce—the main obstacle to your happiness as a couple—taking over as the central plot of your romance. Well, of course his divorce sucks up all the energy in the room. It *is* the main plot line, the big obstacle, which is exactly why you have to make an effort to resist. Stop being a subplot! Be on the lookout for those times that you:

- fail to complain about your day because "he's got so much on his mind"

- excuse his failure to stay current with your work or family concerns

- cancel a plan because he decided that he can see you after all

- put your weekend or holiday plans on hold until you hear from him

- apologize for his behavior to friends or family

- deny feeling resentful when you do

- rationalize his not wanting to hear your feelings or opinions

- know his daily calendar better than your own

2. You feel like a victim.

Kathleen recalls the year of Jim's divorce as her year of living psychosomatically. "I was tired all the time. I thought I had chronic fatigue syndrome. People were always asking me what was wrong. I'd say, well I'm under a lot of stress. It was practically a mantra. I'd fallen down a rabbit's hole, and everything was upside down. Jimmy just kept being not-divorced, no matter how much I tried to be a good girlfriend. Still, the divorce wasn't in sight. We were so very much in love. But that part seemed to last five minutes. And then it was about living in a constant present tense. We couldn't plan a thing, we couldn't look forward to a thing. It was maddening. I felt so beleaguered. I was complaining constantly. It was like, I was forgetting that I'd actually chosen to be in this relationship. This was my choice. It wasn't as if one of us were dying of some terrible disease. It wasn't as if we were living in a war zone. It was a divorce, for god's sake. Was I actually going to just hang in and die trying? I don't think so. I mean, if it were about saving my own child or saving my own marriage, maybe it would be worth running myself into the ground. But not for this. Any day now I was going to start to hate him."

Poor you. You're dating a man who can't quite manage to nail his divorce. We have two words for you: Stop whining. We don't have to remind you that you chose this less-than-wonderful situation, do we? And here are two more words: Stop nagging. Sometimes we don't recognize victimhood when we're in it. We're too panicked, we feel too righteously burdened. We've gotten so low we don't even notice how self-pitying we've become. Watch out for the following:

- When he cancels a plan, you panic.

- When you panic, you say the first thing that comes to your mind ("Oh, my God, do you expect me to be alone on Presidents' Day!") Instead of taking a deep breath and saying the second thing ("Gee, if you're in this much of a bind, I'll just accept that invitation to go skiing in Vail, and we'll get together sometime after the holidays.")

- You fantasize retaliatory behavior, do drive-by's, call him and hang up.

- You can't bear to hear anyone else's happy romantic news.

- You've stopped going to see romantic movies. In fact, you've stopped going to the movies entirely.

- You pick fights with family and friends.

- People have actually come out and told you that they're tired of hearing the same old story.

- Even when your friends say you're absolutely right, you don't feel better.

- You're convinced you have loser karma.

3. You're stuck in the blame-shame cycle, either furious with him or ashamed of yourself.

Beth had a litany of complaints about her boyfriend Henry. They lodged in her throat, somewhere between a scream and a cry. "How could he . . . ?" each one of them began. "What does he think I . . . ?"

they somehow always continued. Beth's friends listened patiently as she explained the Byzantine complexities of the latest chapter of a love affair that had started out so promisingly—Henry was "a couple months" away from finalizing his divorce—but now seemed bogged down in lawyerly logistics and very bad feelings. Why did it seem that Beth always came last: after his kids, his work, his lawyers, his fatigue? Didn't she, Beth, deserve better? Why was his divorce dragging on for close to a year after he'd assured her it was supposed to be over? Who did he think she was, anyway? They'd argue and make up. And Beth would feel shame wash over her. How could she put Henry through this? He was a good man, it wasn't his fault his divorce was taking so long. Anyway, it was all her fault. What was she, Beth, doing in this relationship in the first place? The cycles were exhausting her. She couldn't bear to face her friends and family. So when is he getting divorced? everyone was always asking her. Her parents didn't even mention his name anymore, they were so disgusted.

Does any of that sound like you? When you reach the point where you're ping-ponging between blaming and shaming, consider yourself and your relationship on notice! Blame and shame are a good cop/bad cop melodrama in which you feel compelled to find a victim, whether it's him or yourself. You just careen from one to the other without ever getting out of the box. Blame and shame get you nowhere, so be on the lookout for signs like:

- Inside your own head is a constant dialogue in which you're telling him exactly how he's disappointing you.

- You've begun to lie to friends and family about the status of his divorce.

- When you do express your dissatisfactions to him, you immediately feel remorseful.

- You walk around feeling wronged in general.

- You feel powerless to change things in the relationship.

- Every day feels like worst-case PMS.

- You feel you have no choices.

4. Your good feelings about yourself are dependent on how he's treating you.

Louise's friends could tell the moment she picked up the phone how her relationship with almost-divorced Bernard was going. Louise's voice was a giveaway, her "Hello" alone the barometer of that day's Bernard treatment. And if you called her twice in one evening, you might even get the two-faces-of-Eve effect—a morose Louise at seven, when it looked as though Bernard had to cancel the evening's plans, an ebullient Louise one hour later when he managed to stop by with flowers and a ten-minute hug.

"I'd had episodes of depression in the past. I could feel that emotional weather starting to overtake me," she says now. "I'd been seeing Bernard for close to a year, and he and his wife were in a terrible custody battle. I knew I was in deep water. At that point, I was more worried about myself, frankly, than I was about our relationship. My friends urged me to call my former therapist, and she helped me see that I had some choices."

Louise explained her state of mind to Bernard. "I said, I feel bad about myself when you cancel plans. I feel you don't care about me, and that makes me feel like a fool. I've been through too many rounds of it to feel good about myself. This isn't working for me." Bernard was defensive at first. "I can't make this happen any sooner than it's happening," he told her. "Don't threaten me." Louise didn't let him provoke her. "This isn't an ultimatum," she told him. "But I see where it could feel threatening to you." She asked him not to call her until his agreement with his wife was finally settled.

By the time it was, six months later, Louise had met a wonderful new, never-married man, and was happily involved. Bernard continued to pursue her. Some months later, Louise and Bernard reconnected. His divorce is now finalized. They're making plans to marry.

When a lover feels rejecting, it's tough to maintain your equilibrium. But even worse than a lover who's rejecting is a lover who is sometimes rejecting, sometimes not. Studies indicate that we are more likely to get hooked—and to exhibit the signs of dependent, even obsessive love—when a lover's behavior is a random and unpredictable combination of positive and negative. If you're experiencing your divorcing boyfriend's behavior as this combination of good/bad, you're in danger of victimizing yourself and your relationship. Watch for the following:

- You don't feel right about your life until you check in with him each day.

- If he's unhappy with something you say or do, you feel disproportionately bad about yourself and can't make amends quickly enough.

- If he's more quiet or distant than usual, you assume it has something to do with his feelings about you.

- A sweet word from him suddenly makes you breathe better.

- A disappointing word from him ruins you for the rest of the day.

5. You mood is dependent on his mood. If he's troubled, it brings you down.

"So how are you?" Candy's friend Gail would ask when she called her in the evening. Candy was in love with Al, "the sweetest and most wonderful" man Candy had ever loved. Al had just separated from his wife of eight months, a "mistake marriage" that Candy and Al both treated as a minor stumble on the road to real love, the kind of love Al had discovered with Candy. The trouble was, Al's state of mind was precarious. Although his marriage was brief, the relationship that had preceded it wasn't. Al was handling a huge amount of guilt, which is what Candy explained in excruciating detail to her best friend whenever they spoke. "I'm not so good," Candy told Gail. Deep sigh. "Al had a conversation with his wife's father today. It didn't go well. Al is so depressed. He just wants to be alone tonight." Gail suggested that the two of them catch some dinner, maybe a movie. Deep sigh. "I don't think so," Candy told her. "I'm feeling kind of low. Maybe another time."

Yes, to love another human being is to feel their pain. And if you're a sensitive, empathic kind of person yourself, sensitivity to your loved one's emotional weather is part of the territory of a relationship. Who would want to be in love with someone who *didn't* notice when we were happy, blue, angry, sad? That said, noticing and empathizing with your beloved's emotional state is one thing. Inhabiting that emotional state right along with him is something else entirely. This is getting dangerously close to a relationship too Siamese-twinish to do either one of you any good. When you notice that you "catch" his moods the way the parent of a kindergartner catches colds, you're in trouble. Go ahead and feel his pain and share his joy, but he doesn't need an emotional mimic—and you can't afford to be one. You're relating more to his reality than to your own when you:

- hear your own voice automatically take on the tones of his voice when he expresses distress

- poll your own friends and family for reassurance when he's the one who feels down

- feel as angry at his wife as he does

- hide your own stresses and disappointments from him so as not to "ruin" his good mood

6. Your feelings for him are shifting.

"I'm going to try to make it through the end of the year," Tanya said to herself in August. She'd been dating Sam for just under two years, and had been convinced that on her birthday in June his divorce would be final and she'd have a marriage proposal. Now the summer was almost over, and the simmering resentment she'd been feeling for so along, but especially this angry summer, had deadened into something else.

Tanya had already tried taking a break earlier in the year, suggesting they continue seeing each other but cease being lovers until his "situation" resolved itself. Sam looked pained, but said if it would make things easier for her, he'd go along. The no-sex approach worked for about a month. Now Tanya felt something else happening. When Sam told her about his daughter's rebellious behavior at school, Tanya no longer felt compelled to throw herself into the problem with suggestions, analysis, advice, opinion. Now she said, "I'm sure you'll handle it just fine." It wasn't that she didn't feel sympathetic, she just felt . . . more detached. When Sam complained about stomach aches, she murmured sympathetically, but she didn't jump in as she usually did to insist he see his doctor for that long overdue physical.

"Are you mad about something?" Sam had taken to asking her. "No," she told him. "Not at all." But something was different. Frankly, she felt beyond mad. She felt less connected. Privately, she had put the relationship on notice. Not manipulatively, but organically, protectively, she was beginning to pull back.

Interestingly, things began to change. Little things: Sam went to the doctor without being railroaded into it, then proudly reported back. Bigger things: Sam hired a mediator who helped him and his wife make more progress toward a divorce settlement in two months than two law firms had in a year. That November, they signed the divorce papers. On Christmas, Sam proposed. Tanya never told him how close he'd come to losing her. Somehow, he'd known anyway.

Anger can undermine and erode a love affair, but it isn't the real enemy—indifference is. When you can no longer rouse your emotions enough to feel angry, you're right up against that invisible line. Your feelings are shifting. Put yourself and your relationship on notice—as Tanya did—or you will slip over that invisible line. Beware of the following:

- When he tells you that things are moving along, you roll your eyes.

- You forget where you're supposed to meet for dinner.

- You no longer feel the energy to blame him for the pace of the divorce.

- You feel sorry for him.

- When you list the pros and cons of being his wife, the cons are a lot longer.

- Now he's the one saying, "What's wrong?" and you're the one saying "Nothing."

THE ULTIMATUM

Should you make one? Although every woman's tolerance level is different and unique, overall we discourage making an ultimatum. Our position continues to be, *don't play it safe, play it sane.* We want you to continue to feel freedom of choice. An ultimatum forces you into the ultimate passive position. You're finally betting it all. Yes, sometimes an ultimatum works. We advise against it, not because sometimes it doesn't work, but because it invites a lot of anxiety and a lot of bad feeling into the mix. He feels manipulated. You feel angry. Suddenly it's come down to a prideful power struggle. It's not really fair to him. His divorce involves a person he has no control over. It includes issues of parenthood you have no real connection to.

Rather than challenging him to put up or shut up, inwardly firm up your own timeline. Tell yourself (as Tanya did) that come New Year's or your birthday or September or the first day of summer, you will seriously consider breaking things off if there has been no change. Really, you're the only one who can know what is tolerable and what isn't—not your mother, not your best friend, not him. The best advice someone else will give you about how long to wait can only be based on their own tolerance.

Trust yourself. If you want, you can share your thinking with him. We consider this the modified ultimatum. It's not a threat but a statement of intention. If you still have it in you to deliver it sweetly and lovingly, which is the the only effective way to share your thinking, you haven't crossed that invisible line. You might say this:

I love you, but I don't think I have six more months of waiting for you in me. I know you can't control all the elements of your divorce. I know that you're handling things as best you can. But it's only fair to tell you that I'm running out of gas. I don't want what we share to degenerate into anger or indifference. I'd like to be dating a man available for a permanent commitment. If that isn't our situation by (this summer, my birthday, etc.), I'm going to do my best to move on. I know you don't want to lose me. I trust that you'll do everything in your power to make sure that doesn't happen."

And, as always, it's still up to you to determine what option you'll pursue:

- You can bail out of the relationship.

- You can put the relationship on hold.

- You can continue with the relationship.

DR. LESLIE PAM'S CHAPTER CHECKPOINTS

1. Has he gotten cold feet and started to back away now that his divorce has become final? Don't walk away silently. Say what's on your mind. If he's reneged on a promise to you, let him know how that makes you feel. If you don't, you will be busy having the conversation inside your head for the next three years. People do get scared. It's possible that confronting him with your feelings will even help dislodge him.

2. If he says he's not ready for commitment, don't let him pressure you into an immediate response. Walk away and think about it. Have a good cry. Talk out your feelings with friends. Rehearse or write out what you want to say. Then say it.

3. Don't volunteer to be the one who breaks off the relationship. Some men just start torturing you a little more so as not to be the one to do the dirty work. Don't let that happen. If you take on the difficult job for him, you'll carry your anger about it into your next relationship.

4. It's okay to feel hurt. Hurt heals. You must accept responsibility for having been in the relationship, even if it hasn't worked out. You made the choice. Don't stay stuck in anger. Anger locks you in and prevents healing.

5. Be patient. Healing comes after time. Take your hindsight about the relationship into your next one. Keep loving yourself, and you'll disconnect from his struggle.

CHAPTER TEN

The Girlfriend's
Bill of Rights

O NCE A WOMAN FALLS in love with a separated man, certain truths that ought to be self-evident are often anything but. Between the appealing curve of his biceps and the piercing intelligence of his conversation . . . well, one gets distracted. And before she knows it, she's nibbled at the edges of one conviction, then another—all in the name of companionship or compromise or the pursuit of happiness—only to find she's exchanged certain inalienable rights for certain irresistible pleasures and is just praying that it all comes out all right in the end.

We say if you believe down to your bone marrow that you are entitled to be treated well—even if he's not quite divorced, even if everyone warned you of the risk, even if you knew all the conventional wisdom was stacked against you—the rest is pillow talk. You've won the war. We submit that the following rights are worth fighting—or walking—for. And we urge you to make them as axiomatic a part of your dating gear as your credit card or your mascara, as essential an element in your relationship arsenal as your diaphragm or your best friend. A woman *can* be self-governing in the Republic of Love.

THE RIGHT TO SPEAK FREELY

Free speech doesn't always feel like much of an issue in the early days of love. Infatuation turns us giddy with talk. We are understood! That sublime feeling of merger loosens the tongue as surely as it does the heart. Words flow between you. The very distinction between thought and expression of thought seems to melt away. "Under normal circumstances I'm kind of quiet," says Lanie. When she met Roger, who was making his way through the first months of a separation after a seven-year marriage, speech flourished. "Our first date was a marathon of talk, till three in the morning. Roger was all *about* conversation, so in love with words—and especially *my* words. Everything I thought, felt, observed seemed to captivate him. I couldn't shut up! Finally, a man I could talk to about anything. And he felt the same. He said his marriage had been filled with silence, and that the women he'd been dating since he left he just couldn't really relate to."

So it came as something of a shock when, a month or so into this romance, Lanie discovered she'd mistaken their delirious talkathon for the freedom to speak her mind and heart.

"We hit our first snag—it was about Roger's reluctance to come with me to a family function. My feelings were hurt." And the flow of talk trickled dry. "It was our first out-of-sync moment. I tried to tell him how I felt, and to get him to talk to me about why this was a problem for him, and if it had to do with the status of his divorce or with me—and I could feel him withdraw." Roger turned out to be a wonderful audience, until it came to conflict. "I felt shut down, but our connection was otherwise so wonderful that I let it go"—only to discover that "once you falsify even the smallest part of yourself, you might as well throw in the towel as far as any real intimacy is concerned. The resentment gets too big." Six months later, Lanie broke it off. "The right to speak freely wasn't taken from me. I gave it up. We had no way to develop a vocabulary for sorting through difficult times." Roger called her close to a year later. His divorce was now final. He wanted to try again. Lanie decided to give him another chance. "This time I let him know my misgivings from the start. He said he wanted to change, that he'd do what he could to make change happen." And that was the beginning of a brand-new conversation, one that's still going on. "I helped him listen to me. And now I always feel free to speak."

Consider that freedom the foundation of intimacy. Your words—arranged in conversation, debate, humor, argument—are nothing less than the medium in which you and your man battle for recognition of each other and continue to tell each other exactly how you wish to be appreciated and acknowledged. If there were someone around to read you your rights the moment you fell in love, they'd begin like this: "You have the right to be heard."

THE RIGHT TO REMAIN SILENT

It is also your human right to shut up now and then: to choose *not* to fill all the varieties of silence that exist—should and must exist—between lovers. "Arthur was so woebegotten and guilty during his divorce, so downbeat about everything, I felt it was my duty to be the relationship's cheerleader," says Sonya. "I'd be right there to recognize his mood, describe it, analyze it, sum it up, and prescribe the antidote. Why was it always *my* duty to see the bright side, assume things would work out, put the best spin on every latest development? I felt more like a lobbyist than a girlfriend. I began to think, would I want this job for, like, life? Finally, I gave up. And that's when things actually began to get better. I realized, nobody hired me to do this. And it was true. Arthur needed me to be his lover, not his coach."

It's not your responsibility to verbally manage love. If men could talk, the stories they would tell! Yes, some men do talk. But that still leaves an awful lot who don't—at least, not the talk women think they need to hear, when they need to hear it. The where-is-this-relationship going talk. The you-seem-quiet-is-anything-wrong talk. So we do the talking for love. And sure, filling the silences can promote intimacy by coaxing forth an overdue or difficult conversation. But it can also deprive your relationship of the benefits of silence, encouraging you to become an authority on his inner life rather than your own, forcing you to suggest artificial domains of expertise in your relationship. Love is not another word for I-have-no-unexpressed thoughts. True confessions might get television ratings, but they're not always the ingredients for intimacy. There are times to spill and times to be quiet.

THE RIGHT TO DUE PROCESS

Early in romance, best behavior prevails—on both your parts. Complicating your expectation that you will be treated justly is the inherent inequality of the relationship you're about to embark on: He's not entirely available, you are. Fairness is another issue entirely. As growing intimacy frees you both from artificially good manners, your inclination may be to excuse unfairness, explain it away. You can't tell by looking at a man across a dinner table whether he's willing or able to treat you fairly. It's a wait-and-see kind of thing. "Even when Lewis is displeased about something, or when he's stressed about the divorce, he's even-handed," says Melanie. "He can always see both sides of an issue. Though he may be emotional, he doesn't lose his ability to be fair." Accordingly, Melanie doesn't get defensive. "I trust his regard for me. I know I can always expect to be treated well, despite the extreme conditions of our courtship."

Think of fairness as a more rigorous form of kindness. We can behave kindly toward someone without demanding much of ourselves. Fairness asks us to talk the walk, not just talk the talk. We can be kind, in word or deed, without having to sacrifice anything we feel strongly about. Fairness demands that we actually put our own needs or feelings aside. That's a challenge when a romance is under stress, when one of both of you feels wronged or misunderstood or up against your own limitations. Yet that's exactly the time you must hold tight to this standard and to the expectation that he will honor it as well.

Ask yourself: If he feels wronged, is he still able to hear you out? Are you able to extend the same fairness to him? Fairness isn't a relationship bonus, it's a necessity. Insist on it, or move on.

THE RIGHT TO BE MUDDLED

Granted, love works some miracles—it promotes weight loss, suggests the existence of a higher power, makes you more cheerful around your parents. What love doesn't necessarily do is banish uncertainty. In fact, you might actually discover you occasionally feel more muddled than ever exactly when you seem to have just what you thought you wanted—and that's just fine. You have the right to not always know your own mind, to change your mind, and even now and then to go slightly out of your mind.

"I fell in love with Cal from the first day I met him," says Daisy. "I knew his divorce was a good year off, at least. I felt like I'd found a man I was willing to take that kind of risk for. It didn't seem to matter to me that the divorce would weaken him financially, even emotionally for a while. I loved this guy like crazy. And vice versa. He said he'd get his vasectomy reversed for me. I felt like my best self with him. I thought we'd be an unstoppable team." Then Cal got his divorce. And Daisy felt stricken with indecision.

"The minute the divorce was right there on the horizon, I began to falter. All I could think about suddenly was Cal's debt, Cal's vasectomy, Cal's refusal to go to romantic comedies, Cal's snoring, Cal's three dogs that I wasn't all that crazy about to begin with. I freaked." The day after Cal's divorce papers were signed, he proposed to Daisy. "On his *knees!*" She wept, then turned him down. "I told him that I was mentally ill, but that I needed some time to know him as a divorced person. I wanted more time." He gave it. And that's where they still are, happily and cozily dating, with marriage somewhere, perhaps, in the future.

Why are we so reluctant to admit to romantic uncertainty? When you fall in love with a separated man, there's so much uncertainty out there in the world that you have no control of that you may feel you can't afford to notice any inside yourself. When work or friendship puzzles us, we're perfectly comfortable arranging our ambivalence, indecision, or temporary fogginess into lists of pros and cons, advantages and disadvantages. So why do we feel like idiots when we hit a bout of romantic uncertainty? "I'll feel clearer when Mercury moves out of retrograde," we say instead. Or "I'm under a lot of stress at work." There are times in a love life when decisiveness is the order of the day. But the decision to declare our feelings or to commit to a shared future is often a progression of stops and starts and sudden left turns and the urge to back up and begin again. Why deny it?

Sometimes "I don't know" *is* the most decisive thing you can say to a man. It actually takes confidence to throw up your hands, muffle the control freak in you, and confess the truth. What's freeing about admitting that you don't know with absolute clarity how you feel about a man or whether you're doing the absolute right thing is this: You learn you can act in spite of doubt. Maybe *because* of doubt. "I used to think being changeable was the equivalent of being ditzy," says Amy. "Maybe because Kenny was in the middle of a divorce when we met, he was much more open to doubt and confusion. Weirdly, that suggested a kind of confidence to me. Men I dated in the past needed to be decisive and sure about things. There was no room for gray. The advantage of being an emotional wreck is that it's all gray! I felt freer with Kenny to express second thoughts, doubts, my-stomach-doesn't-feel-right-about-this feelings. Now it's a strength in our marriage. We can always count on one of us to express the I'm-not-sure side of any important decision."

THE RIGHT TO BARE TEETH

Are you pissed off, mad as hell, cranky for no particular reason? Then go ahead and growl—you're entitled. You have a right to feel and express your anger with the man you're sweet on. Sounds simple, but we know it's not always easy. There are so many frustrations—major and minor annoyances in this kind of relationship. And anger always feels riskiest with the people we love. That's because when we choose to express our anger, we trade being liked for acting in our own best interest.

The willingness to brave the repercussions of anger doesn't come naturally to every woman, but we can learn it. Are you reluctant to take a stand on minor issues—saying no to lovemaking, being the plan-maker, last-minute canceling—for fear that it's best to save your energy for the bigger issues surrounding his divorce? We've told you that there are some battles worth fighting and some not. But that's the point: Choose for yourself.

Expressing anger doesn't mean blowing your cork. That kind of hostility only poisons the air of love. But you must recognize your anger inwardly and find a way to communicate it to him in a civil manner—if you choose. Not every man will like your anger. But a man who loves you only when you're smiling isn't up to the demands of real-life romance. "My husband loves my intensity— even when it's not always in his favor," says Lucy, who met him during his separation.

"I fought hard for us to be a couple. He didn't always enjoy it, but he sees it as spunky and passionate." Go ahead and be flexible, but stand firm. And be resolved: In order to form a more perfect union, you will now and again declare hostilities, engage in minor skirmishes, risk civil war. It's your right.

THE RIGHT TO PLEASURE

Everyone knows relationships take work. What we forget from time to time is that they don't require Gulag-level hard labor. When a romance has you feeling as though you work a second job, you've let a critical truth slip from your mind: Love is supposed to make you feel good—good about him and good about yourself; good in bed and out of bed. If you're hanging in, hoping the good part is yet to come, you're on the wrong track. If you're making do because there's no one better, you've talked yourself out of happiness. If pleasure is a sweet but distant memory from the first ten minutes of your love affair, you're playing a fool's game. If you're busting your ass to please him, while feeling precious little in return, if your only pleasure comes from the knowledge that he isn't feeling displeasure, it's time to protest: Your rights are being violated.

"Recently I had an epiphany about a man I've been dating for several months," says Jill. "He's been separated for a little over a year, and his divorce is finally about to happen. We spent the weekend with another couple, and I was kind of stunned at how much more fun they seemed to have with each other. You could see on their faces that they were genuinely glad to see each other when one or the other came in from a walk or an errand. They teased and joked, not just when we all played Pictionary, but when they were cooking dinner and cleaning up. She could put her feet in his lap and expect a willing foot rub. He smiled just watching her defend a conversational point. My boyfriend and I had been together only slightly less long and were talking about living together when his divorce became final, but we didn't have that 'through line' of good feeling. I realized that for us, pleasure was mostly the absence of angst, a lower degree of struggle to stay connected. We have mostly good sex, and we can talk through problems together, but I'm no longer sure that's enough."

That "through line of good feeling" is what tells you, day in and day out, that all the struggling you've done to have this relationship is worth the trouble. We've been seduced by the notion that love can't be expected to go smoothly, but the pleasure-pain scale is still good for evaluating your relationship. Bumps or worse are to be expected. But the difficult times are only worth it if they're outweighed by the good times.

Sexual pleasure, companionable pleasure, and the pleasure that comes from being understood and valued—remind yourself daily that this is your due. Revel in it, demand it, return it in kind. It's love's oxygen. There's nothing character-building about suffering in love. If that's what you're doing, you have a right—and an obligation—to walk the other way.

DR. LESLIE PAM'S CHAPTER CHECKPOINT

You have the right not to give 100 percent of yourself until he is 100 percent available. Protect yourself. Reserve a small piece of yourself, and always hold it back. Make him think about you, wonder about you, try to figure out how he's going to handle you. This kind of withholding is the ultimate act of loving yourself.

APPENDIX A

The Girlfriend's Divorce Primer

WE DON'T SUGGEST YOU immerse yourself in the legalities of his divorce—you've got enough to deal with emotionally. But knowledge is power. Demystify the legal process for yourself so you'll know exactly where he (and, therefore, you) stand in the eyes of the court. Remember that divorce is a matter of public record. If you don't know if he's filed for sure or don't trust the information you've been given, march yourself over to the County Courthouse. You can look it up.

ACTION. A lawsuit.

ADULTERY. Sexual intercourse between a married person and a third party.

AGREEMENT. An oral or written contract, legally enforceable.

ALIENATION OF AFFECTION. Intentional and malicious interference in a marriage.

ALIMONY. Support money which, by court order, must be paid to the spouse.

ANNULMENT. Judgment by a court that, because a marriage was never legally consummated or because it became invalid after the fact, it never existed.

APPEAL. A legal proceeding in which a court's decision is reviewed by a higher court.

APPEARANCE. A defendant's formal submission to the court.

ARBITRATION. A nonjudicial procedure before a neutral third party acting as private judge.

ATTACHMENT. A lien on personal or real property.

BIFURCATION. When the divorce and the financial obligations are tried in separate proceedings.

COHABITATION. Living together without benefit of marriage. Cohabitation during divorce is frowned upon by the courts.

COMMON LAW MARRIAGE. Marriage based on living together, accepted by some states as a legal marriage.

COMMUNITY PROPERTY. Income and property acquired by spouses during their marriage, regardless of whose name it's in, not including that acquired as inheritance or gift.

COMPLAINT (PETITION) FOR DIVORCE. A request to the court for dissolution of a marriage. A complaint states the allegations, identifies the parties, and asks the court to divide property, grant custody, order support.

CONFLICT OF INTEREST (RULES). No lawyer can represent both parties in a divorce. If one spouse interviews a lawyer, shares confidential information, then decides not to retain him, the other spouse is barred from using that lawyer.

CONTESTED DIVORCE. A divorce in which one or more issues hasn't been settled before trial.

CO-RESPONDENT. A person accused of committing adultery with the defendant. Few divorces today name third-party defendants. Adultery is rarely the sole ground for divorce today.

CUSTODY. The legal authority to approve all decisions involving the child.

CUSTODIAL PARENT. The adult with whom the child lives.

DECREE OF DISSOLUTION. The final divorce decree.

DEFENDANT. The spouse who defends against the lawsuit begun by the other spouse.

DEPOSITION. Written testimony under oath and out of court.

DISCOVERY. Formal information-gathering procedures undertaken by lawyers, *i.e.*, request for financial statement; documents; depositions; physical or mental examinations; subpoenas issued to third parties; answers to written questions; inspection of real estate.

DIVORCE DECREE; DECREE OF DISSOLUTION; JUDGMENT OF DIVORCE. The court's final judgment, usually automatic upon termination of the waiting period; a legal divorce.

EQUITABLE DISTRIBUTION. Most states use this system to divide property. Some of the "fair" factors considered: length of the marriage; age, health, occupation of the parties; station in life and life cycle; liabilities and needs; contribution to the marriage (economic, domestic, child-rearing); assets and liabilities; behavior during the marriage; employability and skills.

FAIR AND REASONABLE. The judicial standard for approving marital agreements.

FAULT AND NO-FAULT DIVORCES. Most states have allowed no-fault divorces since the 1970s—meaning, irretrievable breakdown of the marriage with no one spouse considered guilty of marital misconduct. No-fault divorces can be uncontested (the parties present an agreement for the court's approval) or contested (they can't negotiate an agreement and must go to trial). In fault divorces, the complaint specifies the legal basis, or grounds, for divorce: cruel and abusive treatment, adultery, abandonment, etc. Grounds can differ from state to state.

FILE. A document submitted to and officially received by the court.

FIND; FINDINGS. The conclusions of the court or jury after interpreting the evidence.

GROUNDS FOR DIVORCE. The legal basis for a divorce, according to state statutes.

INJUNCTION. A court order that prohibits certain activity. An affirmative injunction in a divorce case usually relates to child visitation.

JOINT CUSTODY. A form of custody in which both parents share responsibilities and decision-making relative to minor children.

JOINT PROPERTY. Property held in the name of more than one person.

LEGAL SEPARATION. A lawsuit for support while the spouses remain living separately, but no divorce judgement is granted to end the marriage.

LUMP SUM ALIMONY. Spousal support in a single payment or in a fixed amount paid in installments.

MAINTENANCE. Alimony.

MARITAL PROPERTY. All income and property acquired by spouses during a marriage, except gifts and inheritances.

MEDIATION. A voluntary process in which a neutral third party works with a divorcing couple to develop a separation agreement. Mediation requires mutual trust and cooperation, since full financial disclosure is required and mediation is discontinued if either party refuses to continue. Each spouse has his or her lawyer review the agreement before it is signed.

MOTION. A request to the court, either written or oral, for some particular relief: temporary support, more complete discovery, etc.

NEGOTIATED SETTLEMENT; NEGOTIATED AGREEMENT. A separation agreement, developed without third-party mediation or arbitration.

ORDER; COURT ORDER; ORDER OF THE COURT. The court's written ruling on a particular matter.

PALIMONY. Payment of support by one unmarried lover to another.

PREMARITAL ASSETS. Assets acquired before marriage. In equitable distribution states these assets are considered part of the marital estate; in community property states, they are considered separate property.

PRENUPTIAL AGREEMENT. A premarital contract that specifies the rights and responsibilities of the parties upon death and divorce. A prenup must be fair and reasonable at the time entered. The longer a marriage, the less enforceable it becomes.

PRIVILEGE. The right of evidence, based on certain confidential communications, to be excluded.

PROBATE. The legal process of administering an estate after death.

REHABILITATIVE ALIMONY. Short-term spousal support to help recipient begin a new life.

SANCTIONS. Established to allow courts to punish uncooperative and obstructionist behavior.

SEPARATE PROPERTY. Property owned by one spouse and not considered part of the marital estate.

SETOFF. A debt of one spouse which is deducted by the court from the debt of the other spouse.

SOLE CUSTODY. When one parent is given physical custody of the child and the right to make all decisions regarding the child's upbringing.

SPLIT CUSTODY. When physical custody is split between the parties.

STAY; STAY OF PROCEEDINGS. The stopping of a judicial proceeding.

SUBPOENA. A document served by the court upon a person not directly involved in a lawsuit, requiring that person to appear and give testimony at a deposition or a court hearing.

SUMMONS. A document served by the court notifying the defendant that a complaint has been filed and he or she must respond.

VACATE THE MARITAL HOME, MOTION TO. A request to the court (usually by the wife) asking that one party (usually the husband) be forced to leave the marital home.

VISITATION. The right of a parent who does not have physical custody to visit the child.

A State-by-State Guide
to Divorce Laws

ALABAMA. Permits most forms of no-fault as well as fault divorces. A separate property state. Must be a resident for six months before you can obtain a divorce.

ALASKA. Permits traditional fault divorces. Does not permit "irreconcilable differences" no-fault divorces. Does permit incompatibility and mutual consent decrees. A separate property state. Must be a bona fide Alaska resident to obtain a divorce.

ARIZONA. Permits "irreconcilable differences" no-fault divorces and mutual consent decrees. Does not permit fault divorces. A community property state. Must reside for 90 days to obtain a divorce.

ARKANSAS. Permits fault divorces. Permits a no-fault divorce if you've lived separate and apart for 3 years. A separate property state. Must be a resident for 60 days to obtain a divorce.

CALIFORNIA. Only permits "irreconcilable difference" no-fault divorces and mutual consent decrees. A community property state. Must be a resident for 6 months to obtain a divorce.

COLORADO. Permits "irreconcilable differences" no-fault divorces and mutual consent decrees. Does not permit fault divorces. A separate property state. Must live in the state for 90 days to obtain a divorce.

CONNECTICUT. Permits fault divorces and most forms of no-fault divorce, including "irreconcilable differences" and living separate and apart. Must live in the state for one year to obtain a divorce.

DELAWARE. Permits fault divorces and "irreconcilable differences" and incompatibility forms of no-fault divorce. A separate property state. Must live in the state for 6 months to obtain a divorce.

DISTRICT OF COLUMBIA. Permits fault divorces. Permits no-fault divorces based on living separate and apart for 1 year or 6 months voluntary separation. A separate property jurisdiction. Residency requirement: 6 months.

FLORIDA. Permits fault divorces and "irreconcilable differences" no-fault divorces. A separate property state. Must live in the state for 6 months to obtain a divorce.

GEORGIA. Permits fault divorces and "irreconcilable differences" no-fault divorces. A separate property state. Must live in the state for 6 months to obtain a divorce.

HAWAII. Permits "irreconcilable differences" no-fault divorces and divorces based on living separate and apart and mutual consent decrees. Does not permit fault divorces. A separate property state. Must live in Hawaii for 6 months to obtain a divorce.

IDAHO. Permits fault divorce and no-fault divorces based on "irreconcilable differences" or living separate and apart. A community property state. Must live in Idaho for 6 weeks to obtain a divorce.

ILLINOIS. Permits no-fault divorce based on "irretrievable breakdown in the marriage" and living separate and apart for 2 years. Permits mutual consent divorces if parties have been living apart for 6 months. Permits fault divorces. A separate property state. Must live in the state for 90 days to obtain a divorce.

INDIANA. Permits "irreconcilable differences" no-fault divorces only. A separate property state. Must live in the state for 6 months to obtain a divorce.

IOWA. Permits "irreconcilable differences" no-fault divorces only. A separate property state. Must live in the state one year to obtain a divorce.

KANSAS. Permits incompatibility no-fault divorces and fault divorces. A separate property state. Must live in the state 60 days to obtain a divorce.

KENTUCKY. Permits incompatibility no-fault divorces and fault divorces. A separate property state. Must live in the state 180 days to obtain a divorce.

LOUISIANA. Permits fault divorces and no-fault divorces based on living separate and apart for 6 months. A community property state. Residency requirement: 1 year.

MAINE. Permits no-fault divorces based on "irreconcilable differences" and fault divorces. A separate property state. Residency requirement: 6 months.

MARYLAND. Permits no-fault divorces based on living separate and apart for 1 year. Permits fault divorces. A separate property state. Residency requirement: 1 year when both parties agree.

MASSACHUSETTS. Permits no-fault divorces based on "irreconcilable differences" if the parties sign a marital settlement agreement. Permits fault divorces. A separate property state. Residency requirement: 1 year.

MICHIGAN. Permits only "irreconcilable differences" no-fault divorces. A separate property state. Residency requirement: 6 months, but 1 year if the marriage breakdown arose out of the state.

MINNESOTA. Permits no-fault divorces only, based on "irreconcilable differences" or living separate and apart for 180 days. A separate property state. Residency requirement: 180 days.

MISSISSIPPI. Permits fault divorces. Permits "irreconcilable differences" no-fault divorces. A separate property state. Residency requirement: 6 months.

MISSOURI. Permits fault divorces. Permits "irreconcilable differences" no-fault divorces. A separate property state. Residency requirement: 90 days.

MONTANA. Permits no-fault divorces based on "irreconcilable differences" or living separate and apart for 180 days. Does not permit fault divorce. A separate property state. Residency requirement: 90 days.

NEBRASKA. Permits no-fault divorces based on "irreconcilable differences" only. Does not permit fault divorces. A separate property state. Residency requirement: 1 year.

NEVADA. Permits fault divorces. Permits no-fault divorces based on incompatibility or living separate and apart for 1 year. A community property state. Residency requirement: 6 weeks.

NEW HAMPSHIRE. Permits fault divorces. Permits no-fault divorces based on "irreconcilable differences." A separate property state. Residency requirement: 1 year.

NEW JERSEY. Permits fault divorces. Permits no-fault divorces based on living separate and apart for 18 months. A separate property state. Residency requirement: 1 year.

NEW MEXICO. Permits fault divorces. Permits no-fault divorces based on incompatibility. A community property state. Residency requirement: 6 months.

NEW YORK. Permits fault divorces. Permits no-fault divorces based on a judicial separation for 1 year or more. A separate property state. Residency requirement: 1 year.

NORTH CAROLINA. Permits fault divorces. Permits no-fault divorces based on living separate and apart for 1 year. A separate property state. Residency requirement: 6 months.

NORTH DAKOTA. Permits fault divorces. Permits "irreconcilable differences" no-fault divorces. A separate property state. Residency requirement: 6 months.

OHIO. Permits fault divorces. Permits no-fault divorces based on incompatibility and living separate and apart for 1 year and mutual consent decrees. A separate property state. Residency requirement: 6 months.

OKLAHOMA. Permits fault divorces. Permits no-fault divorces based on incompatibility. A separate property state. Residency requirement: 6 months.

OREGON. Permits no-fault divorces based on "irreconcilable differences" or mutual consent. A separate property state. Residency requirement: 6 months.

PENNSYLVANIA. Permits fault divorces. Permits no-fault divorces based on "irreconcilable differences" or living separate and apart for 2 years. A separate property state. Residency requirement: 6 months.

RHODE ISLAND. Permits fault divorces. Permits no-fault divorces based on "irreconcilable differences" or living separate and apart for 3 years. A separate property state. Residency requirement: 1 year.

SOUTH CAROLINA. Permits fault divorces. Permits no-fault divorces based on "irreconcilable differences" or living separate and apart for 1 year. A separate property state. Residency requirement: 1 year. If both parties live in state: 3 months.

SOUTH DAKOTA. Permits fault divorces. Permits "irreconcilable differences" no-fault divorces. A separate property state. Residency requirement: From the time the action is commenced until the action is concluded.

TENNESSEE. Permits fault divorces. Permits no-fault divorces based on "irreconcilable differences" and living separate and apart for 3 years. A separate property state. Residency requirement: 6 months.

TEXAS. Permits fault divorces. Permits no-fault divorces based on living separate and apart for 3 years. A community property state. Residency requirement: 6 months.

UTAH. Permits fault divorces. Permits no-fault divorces based on "irreconcilable differences" or living separate and apart for 3 years. A separate property state. Residency requirement: 90 days.

VERMONT. Permits fault divorces. Permits no-fault divorces based on living separate and apart for 6 months. A separate property state. Residency requirement: 6 months.

VIRGINIA. Permits fault divorces. Permits no-fault divorces based on living separate and apart for 6 months. A separate property state. Residency requirement: 6 months.

WASHINGTON. Permits no-fault divorces based on "irreconcilable differences" or mutual consent. A community property state. Divorce available to residents only, no time requirement.

WEST VIRGINIA. Permits no-fault divorces based on "irreconcilable differences" or living separate and apart for 1 year. A separate property state. Residency requirement: 1 year.

WISCONSIN. Permits no-fault divorces based on "irreconcilable differences" or mutual consent. A separate property state. Residency requirement: 6 months.

WYOMING. Permits fault divorces. Permits no-fault divorces based on "irreconcilable differences." A separate property state. Residency requirement: 60 days.